Getting Out
From Under

Also by Stephanie Winston

Getting Organized

The Organized Executive

Stephanie Winston's Best Organizing Tips

Getting Out From Under

Redefining Your Priorities in an Overwhelming World

A Powerful Program for Personal Change

Stephanie Winston

PERSEUS BOOKS
Reading, Massachusetts

Library of Congress Catalog Card Number: 98-89425

ISBN 0-7382-0098-0

Perseus Books is a member of the Perseus Books Group

Text design by Joyce C. Weston
Set in 11-point Sabon by Joyce C. Weston

1 2 3 4 5 6 7 8 9—0302010099
First printing, February 1999

Perseus Books are available at special discounts for bulk purchases in the U.S. by corporations, institutions, and other organizations. For more information, please contact the Special Markets Department at HarperCollins Publishers, 10 East 53rd Street, New York, NY 10022, or call 1-212-207-7528.

Find us on the World Wide Web at
http://www.aw.com/gb/

To my sisters,

Terry Pickett and Dinah Lovitch

Contents

Acknowledgments

My warm thanks to Catherine Whitney for her insightful editorial feedback, her help in smoothing out the rough edges of my ideas and my prose, and her always intelligent, always sound advice. This book would not have been possible without her.

Marnie Patterson Cochran is the Perseus Books senior editor whose enthusiasm for the project, sensitivity to its nuances, and editorial guidance served as a compass throughout.

Appreciation to Paul Krafin, Janet Schuler, and JoAnn and David Klein, whose contributions added a great deal.

And thanks to literary agent extraordinaire Jane Dystel, who pulled all the pieces together and made it work.

Getting Out From Under

The Crisis of Time

When I wrote my first book, *Getting Organized,* I was responding to the need people have to get a semblance of control over the external chaos in their lives—the stuff in their closets and the stuff on their schedules that is bogging them down.

I've noticed, however, that over the past few years a different and seemingly deeper crisis has emerged. Those same people for whom gaining control over their papers and their closets was enough ten or fifteen years ago now find that their *crisis of time* is not simply solved by getting more organized. The clutter they experience is as much *internal* as external— the result of having too many conflicting choices, a growing list of priorities to shuffle in the same time frame, and a burgeoning affliction of guilt and disappointment at not being able to handle everything perfectly.

When I started investigating why people were having such difficulty getting out from under, I discovered that this era of opportunity has had the adverse effect of adding layers of responsibility. The birth of new possibilities has given rise to the birth of new "shoulds," doubling the intensity of already crowded lives. These "shoulds" are reinforced by an ever-widening cadre of experts discoursing in every public medium about what it means to be a good parent, a productive employee, an appealing personality, a beautiful woman or man, a go-getter in business, a person of spiritual depth, a perfect specimen of physical fitness and health—and still have time to plant petunias.

The imperatives blast daily from car radios and television talk shows. Newspapers are so chock-full of the voices of advice and warning—on everything from diet to pet care—that there's barely room for the news. The impossible ideals of both men's and women's fitness and fashion magazines haunt us wherever we go. A friend of mine told me that she feels Martha Stewart staring disapprovingly from the supermarket magazine rack as she tries to sneak by with her frozen dinners. The result is the feeling of being suffocated by all the layers that keep getting added to society's proposed priority pile.

It seems to me that there are several underlying reasons for the new crisis of time, including:

- Having too many values to which you've assigned equal priority.
- Negative attitudes about sharing or delegating responsibility.
- The inability to say no, or close doors once they're opened.
- Making important choices using vaguely defined reasoning.
- The fear of being judged as inadequate.

I liken the panic many people experience to being buried in an avalanche of snow. They paw furiously to escape—even though they have no idea which direction leads to freedom. They are driven by a survival instinct but are working blind. The same is true of many people who are simply overwhelmed as they scramble to define time for work, family, partners, children, community, and themselves. Often their attempts to escape the morass lead to panic-stricken flailing.

Panic, in turn, usually leads to rash, ill-informed decisions. Actions become *reactive*, rather than *proactive*. Too frantic to consider realistic solutions, many people throw up their hands and cry, "That does it! I'm quitting my job," or, "What a rat race! I'm moving to the country," or, "This is too much. Let's sell the house, and too bad if we burn our bridges." The problem with burning bridges, as we all know, is that they stay burned; you can't go back. But this is the result of building a full head of steam—the tendency to explode spontaneously rather than to reflect on your dilemma and establish realistic goals.

One way this spontaneous rebellion is being expressed constructively is in the movement known as "voluntary simplicity." There has been a surge in the popularity of the concept of simplifying your life, and the fascination is understandable. In an era when people generally have too many possessions and too many obligations, this trend reflects a desire to escape the enormous complexity of today's world. The clutter of packed schedules leaves little time for the depressurizing pleasures so crucial to a balanced existence. More often than not, the longing to run away from it all, to fold up the tent and escape, is more a fantasy than a realistic goal. The yearning for simplicity may just be a sign that you need to pause and reflect about what you really want—to reconnect with long-lost dreams and ideals.

How are you going to do *that* when you're so far in over your head that you barely have enough mental energy to function, much less the time needed for reflective thought?

As an organizer, I'm often consulted when the crush of time and responsibility becomes too much to bear. One of my clients spoke for many when he quietly stated, "I just want to get back to the basics." That is a big part of the need people are experiencing. Many adults are searching for a memory of who they were and what they cared about before all the layers got heaped on. They're longing for a better and more fulfilling way of *using* the time they have—instead of being *used* by time. The disorganization in their plan for the future gets translated into a daily disorganization—and ultimately a feeling of having little control over their destiny.

In my experience, people who are disorganized are *scared*. They don't know why they can't get it together, and they don't know how to take the first step. It's as if they're standing outside the problem. My approach is to bring them into focus and help them take that first step—even if it's a small step.

In the process of engaging, they begin to see that getting out from under is not an impossible goal. Lest you think I'm just another "expert" piling on rules to live by, let me assure you that my method is very different from simply passing along advice. Advice is passive. It may provide a road map, but it doesn't ride in the car with you, and it doesn't always get you where you want to go. There is a series of strategies I've developed that will actively engage you in tangible measures you can begin to take right now to get out from under.

A Road Map to Change

Getting Out From Under offers a rather unconventional way of approaching change in your life. When you're really in a state of time crisis, the first imperative is getting some room to breathe. On a very practical level, you need to open up some time and space in your daily life. Let's practice time triage. Deal with the emergency first. Once it's over and you're breathing, we'll look at making changes that will keep you out of danger.

Part I, "Room to Breathe," will give you some basic tools you can use right away. In fact, you may be one of those lucky individuals who needs nothing more than that. However, many people I encounter in my work are in need of a deeper change. The question is—what kind of a change? A new career? A move? A shift in marital status? Part II, "Examine Your Personal Universe," will help you answer that question. Many people have found the Solar System Technique outlined here to be a comprehensive and exhilarating method for examining their lives. You'll find out who you are and what you really want. Armed with your new insights, you can then explore Part III, which will enable you to open up your universe and consider practical options in a way that you may not have realized was possible.

The end goal is to arm you with the tools you need to make any change in your life. A friend once confided, "My deepest fear is that I'll wake up at age sixty and feel that most of my life has passed me by while I was busy trying to keep up." I knew what she was talking about.

Long ago, I decided that I wouldn't let that happen to me, and, in doing so, I'd find a way to help others facing the same circumstances. What follows has worked for me, and for countless others. You don't have to fear waking up one day wondering where the hopes, dreams, and desires of your life have gone. By using the Solar System Technique, you can identify them and learn to reactivate those aspects of your life that haven't been receiving enough of your time and attention.

PART I

Room to Breathe

CHAPTER 1

Clearing the Underbrush

How to Add an Extra Hour to Your Day

My friend Mary recently came home from work to find that a pipe had begun leaking under her kitchen sink, causing quite a mess. Already overwhelmed by the demands of her career and raising three boys, Mary felt herself start to panic. She desperately grabbed the phone book and called the first plumber on the list. He came, evaluated the problem, and told Mary she needed a new trap system and pipes under the sink. He found a pipe about to let go in her bathroom, as well. He estimated the total cost of repairs at about $650—a figure that made Mary shake her head in disbelief. But she needed the job done, so she signed the contract and gave the plumber what he asked for as a down payment—$300.

Later, when Mary phoned her mother and told her about what had transpired, her mother expressed horror to learn that she'd signed a contract with the first plumber she'd called. "You don't even know if he's reputable. How could you sign a contract before you checked out other plumbers?"

Mary sighed resignedly. "Mom, I don't care. As long as it gets done."

Her mother didn't understand. "You'd rather pay an exorbitant price than spend a few minutes on the phone," she chided. Mary couldn't find a way to explain that it was so much more than that.

Mary's mother would describe the situation this way: "My daughter just *couldn't be bothered* to shop around for the best deal." But Mary saw it differently. In the crush of her life, she literally didn't have the emotional time to worry about it, much less the *physical* time to interview plumbers. Rationally, she knew that she had handled the matter sloppily, and she felt guilty about not looking for a better price, but she just *couldn't*.

Mary's story perfectly demonstrates the churning internal dynamics of the crisis of time. Time is not just a matter of minutes and how you spend them. Time is something you experience all of a piece. When someone pressures you by saying, "It will take only a few minutes," or "Can't you spare a half hour?" you hear the request as a far greater claim on your time and psyche than the actual minutes might imply.

That's why the first order of business—and the focus of Part I—is to find some breathing room. Then you can reflect on your future, reinforced with a full tank of oxygen.

The most common reactions I hear are breathless declarations along the lines of:

"My day is so jam-packed, I don't even have the five minutes it takes to figure out how to be more organized."

"Panic is my middle name."

"I'm so busy doing, I don't have time to write a 'To Do' list."

"I'm always late—it's the only way I can stay ahead of myself."

And the most common plea of all is "I need another hour in my day!" Unfortunately, no extra hours are available. What is *really* needed is a way to free up a few of the twenty-four hours already on the clock. You need time and space to breathe. This can be done—and that's a promise.

Flash! How to Make Some Changes Right Now

Let's start with the basics: *Right now, this minute,* what can you do to ease the pressures of an overly hectic life? You don't have time to think about it or analyze it. You need a series of highly specific strategies you can employ *now* that will give you a little extra time each day.

This is what I call "*flash organizing.*" It's immediate and practical. The techniques include organizing tips for individuals and businesses. These tips have the effect of pumping oxygen directly into your brain and clearing your mind. These flash organizing tips can help to provide you with the time and breathing space you so desperately need.

The 10% Solution

Sometimes the most significant gains in our free time emerge from the smallest of the changes we decide to make in our lives. Even a 10% change can make a big difference. That's why I call it the "10% Solution."

Nancy is an editor at a publishing company that had always had a relaxed attitude about morning arrivals. Anything up to 9:45 A.M. was considered on time—which was fine with Nancy because she is resolutely *not* a morning person. Nancy's schedule was placed in jeopardy when a new managing editor suddenly requested that everyone be in the office by 9 A.M. Nancy imagined she'd need to be up before dawn to make her new work hours possible. She felt that her heretofore untested skill at early reveille was about to be put to use.

Forty-five minutes—the difference between arriving at work

WHAT'S YOUR CHAOS QUOTIENT?

Do you deliberately call people when you know you'll get their answering machines because you don't have time to talk?

Are you often late paying bills because you forget about them?

Does the idea of being sick in bed for a day drive you to despair?

Do you often have trouble putting your hands on a phone number or a memo when you need it?

Do you have a hard time remembering the last time you had a relaxing lunch with a friend?

Do your vacation days tend to pile up every year because you don't have time to take them?

Do you have magazines and newspapers that are more than a month old that you keep "meaning to read"?

Do you ever forget appointments?

Do you have a hard time saying no when someone asks for a moment of your time?

Score: If you answered yes to three or fewer, you're in basically good health. If you answered yes to between four and six, you need an immediate checkup. If you answered yes to seven or more, emergency CPR is required.

at 9:00 A.M., and arriving at 9:45 A.M. Three-quarters of an hour. But for Nancy, with a family of five to get out the door, this crisis of time posed a real challenge. Her immediate solution was obvious—she had to start getting up earlier. The very thought made Nancy shudder.

But there is another way—THE 10% SOLUTION.

I asked Nancy to think about everything she did in the morning, even to write it down. Then I asked her to find ways to do it 10% faster, 10% more efficiently, and if possible, eliminate 10% of the items on the list. I explained to Nancy that it's often the small, incremental improvements—doing something the night before, saving a few steps here and there—that really add up to big payoffs. Nancy was dubious, but agreed to try the idea and see how it worked out.

About five weeks later, Nancy called to tell me that making small, 10% modifications in her family's morning routine had yielded some terrific dividends. She was getting out of bed only 10 minutes earlier, but she hadn't been late for work even once. Even better was the new attitude that had come with the changes. The whole family was washed, dressed, fed, and out the door every morning with less stress than ever before. In addition to rising 10 minutes earlier, here are the changes that Nancy made:

- Breakfast preparations are done the night before. When Nancy walks into the kitchen in the morning, the coffee is ready to be made, orange juice is already prepared, the bread is by the toaster, and the table is set, including the cereal. All Nancy does is flip a couple of switches and bring out the jam, butter, and milk. Incidentally, the kitchen preparation is her husband Seth's nightly contribution to the changes they've instituted.

- Each of the three children—Ricky, Susan, and Jessica—gets their clothing for the next day ready. Socks, shoes, shirts, underwear, pants, skirts—everything is laid out the night before.

- Everything gets placed by the door. Before bedtime, the kids pack their bookbags and line them up in the hallway by the front door. Nancy and Seth do the same with their briefcases. If dry cleaning needs to be dropped off or shoes repaired, these items get placed there as well.

- To simplify bed making, Nancy has switched from bed-spreads to duvets, which can be easily arranged to make each bed in less than a minute.

Nancy is pleased with almost every change. But, like a lot of people, she prefers showering in the morning. It helps to wake her up. Unfortunately, she discovered that she could save seventeen minutes in the morning if she showered the night before. So, her refreshing daily wake-up showers have been banished to the realm of weekend pleasures. It's Nancy's only complaint about the 10% Solution.

Using Nancy's experience as your guide, take any process that seems to be overcomplicated or that takes too long, and break it down into three to five elements. Then figure out how you can reduce or eliminate one of the elements. For example, a friend of mine found that preparations for the Christmas holidays were becoming overwhelming. She broke down her holiday obligations into four areas: sending cards, buying and wrapping gifts, decorating a tree, and preparing Christmas dinner for the extended family. She then reduced her Christmas card list by eliminating everyone she hadn't communicated with in the past two years. She was able to cut down on her shopping and wrapping by giving some gift certificates. She announced that Christmas dinner was going to be a potluck, thus reducing her time in the kitchen. The result was that the holiday became much more manageable and enjoyable. When you begin to think incrementally, you'll be surprised at the *big* difference *small* changes can make.

Streamlining Your Space

Now, let's be bold, and take a more thorough and focused look at ways to massage some of the knots out of specific pressure points in your life. If we apply our simplifying and organizing

QUICK HOME TIME SAVERS

Creat a "buddy basket," and place in it all papers to be discussed with your partner—bills, an invitation, report cards. Make a date to talk things over and clean the basket out twice a week.

Keep a separate basket or file of quick things to flip through: recipes you want to file, catalogs, alumni or school notes, local newsletters, or any other reading material you can handle while you're holding on the phone or waiting for the water to boil.

If you're deluged with catalogs, don't even bring them into the house. Tear out the catalog pages you're interested in, plus the order form, while you're still standing at the mailbox! Throw the rest of the catalog away. You can then make any purchasing decisions at your leisure. (You can reduce your unwanted mail by writing to Stop the Mail, P.O. Box 9008, Farmingdale, NY 11735-9008. Ask that your name not be sold to mailing list companies.)

Did you just buy your *third* bottle of rosemary because you didn't know you had any? A less drastic solution than joining your local Rosemary Recovery Group might be to alphabetize your spices, from arrowroot to turmeric. I know it seems deceptively simple, but it works!

techniques to those sore spots, we'll be able to begin releasing the constant press of both time and space. As a result, you'll feel calmer because you'll *be* calmer.

No one's asking you to attain a sudden state of total serenity and deep Zen-like concentration and calm. The idea is to have everything you want and need, and to want and need everything you have.

Want and need everything you have? We're not really used

to thinking that way. The truth is that most people are accu-
mulators—we hang onto things that "cost too much" for the
space they take up and the pleasure they bring. In this respect,
your *space* can be a factor in your crisis of time.

So, how do you go about deciding whether something gives
you enough pleasure to warrant the space it takes up in your
life? First of all, there is no right or wrong answer. However, I've
found that merely by focusing on the question—perhaps for the
first time ever—you'll begin to find an answer for yourself.

Begin with this simple exercise. Choose a room in your
house and write down the items in it. For example:

LIVING ROOM
sofa
chair
bookcase
great-grandmother's armoire
TV stand and TV

When you have completed your list, take each item, one at
a time, and ask yourself several questions. For the purposes of
this example, let's take great-grandmother's armoire.

- What is the net pleasure vs. the net aggravation or irrita-
  tion? Does great-grandmother's armoire give enough pleasure that the time it takes to keep it dusted and polished is
  worthwhile? If you *want* the armoire, lovely; or is it there
  because you can't think of what else to do with it?

- What is the practical cost/benefit in terms of time and
  space? Does great-grandmother's armoire serve a function?
  Could this space be better used for something else, such as
  extra tables or chairs? For that matter, would just opening
  up the space and putting nothing else in it be a net plus?

- Is there a "peace of mind" factor? Does great-grandmother's armoire have a soothing effect on you, eliciting fond memories of the past? Or did you not much care for great-grandmother, anyway?

As you begin to ask these questions, it will become easier to make real choices about what adds to your net pleasure, and what detracts from it.

Apply the same kind of thinking to the couch, chairs, and other items in the room. For instance, if you have pets or young children, is the couch easy-care, or could it be made so with the addition of a throw? Are people forever balancing their drinks on the arms of the chairs because there aren't enough end tables? Bottom line: Seek out comfort and convenience.

It can be an immensely satisfying and liberating experience to have identified the major things that take up your time and space, evaluating the level of pleasure and utility they provide, and deciding whether they warrant their cost in time and effort. It's an immediate result that underscores your determination to take control over your life. It also helps to simply illustrate some of the more complex choices you'll have the opportunity to make later in the book.

Cutting a Swath Through Paper and Time

If you've already used some of my tips for managing your personal crisis of time—flash organizing and simplifying pressure points—then you've started to experience some of the benefits of a fundamentally organized life. In this section we'll be looking at two major aspects of the organized life that prove especially onerous—paper management and time management.

There are some simple ideas that will untangle and demystify these sometimes unnecessarily convoluted processes. You'll soon be in total command.

PLAY THE DISASTER GAME

This exercise is designed to help you look at all of your material possessions from a new perspective. There's nothing like a disaster to help you let go of what isn't important to you. The countless Americans who have undergone the trials of floods, tornadoes, hurricanes, and fires can certainly attest to that. Hopefully, you'll be lucky enough to do this exercise without being forced to because of actual circumstance.

Challenge: You've just been told you have to leave your home, and you can salvage only what you can fit in your car. You have five minutes to decide what you'll take.

Conquering the Paper Tiger

We've all seen desks covered with papers, files, catalogs, and more. Indeed, we may actually *have* them. Whether it's your desk at the office or at home, it's easy to get discouraged. Piles seem to grow on piles. The basic disorder begins to symbolize your other feelings as well—as though you're weighed down by everything else in life. On the other hand, a desk where all the papers have been dealt with sends a very different message. Order, control, discipline, calm. It makes you feel, "If I can do this, then I can gain a degree of mastery over other aspects of my life as well!"

There's one common misunderstanding that nearly everyone shares when it comes to organizing a desk: It's not a problem of *neatness*; it's a problem of *decision making*. I call it the Chinese-water-torture version of decision making, because every little scrap of paper, every phone number scribbled on the back of an envelope, needs to have a decision made about it. That can feel intimidating, especially if you're pressed for time.

So here's what tends to happen: A piece of paper comes into your life—be it an interoffice memo, letter, e-mail printout, or fax. In the busy rush of the day, you're apt to glance at it and say to yourself, "Well, I'm not quite sure what to do with this right now. So I'll place it neatly on top of the pile on the right side of my desk and think about it tomorrow." Famous last words. People have been thinking about tomorrow forever—famously. Think of gorgeous Vivien Leigh, in *Gone with the Wind,* poutily proclaiming "Tomorrow is another day." I call this the "Scarlett O'Hara Syndrome."

How many tomorrows before those papers that have been relegated to the side of your desk shift precipitously, causing carefully stacked piles to scatter everywhere? It doesn't take long, as you know.

There are *only* four decisions you can make about a piece of paper: You can *toss* it; you can *refer* it, which means passing it along or discussing it with someone else; you can *act* on it personally; or you can *file* it. In fact, I've turned this into an acronym—the TRAF system.

Toss.

I would seriously encourage you to toss as many papers as you reasonably can. If you're not certain, ask if you can find a duplicate in the unlikely event you'll need it. If so, then throw it away.

```
TRAF

TOSS

REFER

ACT

FILE
```

Refer.

This means there's someone else you want to share this information with, so you'll refer it to them. Maybe you got a notice concerning a seminar. It's not your thing, but you have a friend who might be interested. So, pass it on. You may want to go over a memo with your

---

HOW A TOP EXECUTIVE ORGANIZES
WITH TRAF

A few years ago, I had the opportunity to spend the day with John Curley, CEO of the Gannett Corporation. When it came time to go through his mail, Curley expedited it efficiently, spontaneously using a system similar to TRAF. Let's watch:

TOSS: An informational form letter from NBC, an invitation to a fundraiser, flight schedules for executives.

REFER: A résumé, information on a mini-sabbatical program for Gannett News staff members.

ACT: A letter from an Eastern European newspaper interested in investment, a group of letters for signature, the Executive News Summary distributed daily to Gannett execs (which he read and then tossed).

FILE: A memo about advertising in Detroit, a complaint letter, the agenda for an upcoming meeting, a financial report.

---

boss relating to the new software you're buying, or discuss it with a colleague.

Here's a tip for dealing with the "refers" at the office. Make a file for each of the people you interact with the most— your boss, an assistant, a couple of your office mates—and pop it into that person's folder. When there's an opportunity to go over things, you can pull out that person's folder and say, "Here are a few things that we need to discuss"—and go over them together.

Act.

This is the category for all the notes, memos, and mail you receive that you need to personally respond to in some way, such as analyzing those figures, purchasing more supplies, getting the statistics together to back up your monthly report, and responding to that query.

Keep all of your action papers in one place, and give yourself a generous half hour each day to deal with them. If you're afraid that if you file them, you'll forget them, then it's perfectly all right to leave them out on your desk. Keep them in the same place, though, as a prompt to you.

File.

File-as-you-go is a surefire way to prevent a buildup of articles and materials that you eventually intend to file. The real trick to filing is to make the file headings as clear as you can and easy to remember. It all depends on your line of work, of course. Under a title like Business Catalogs–June, I'd combine all the catalogs that arrived in June that directly pertain to my business needs. If the Business Catalogs–June file isn't gone through and acted on by the third week in June, toss it out.

It's the small decisions you make that often have the most effect on your time management, efficiency, and productivity. TRAFing is simple, but you'll see major results. In fact, I'll make you a promise: If you'll start spending fifteen minutes a day TRAFing the current day's incoming mail, memos, and faxes, you'll soon have gained mastery over your papers. It will probably take a couple of weeks to clear up past materials that built up before you started implementing the TRAF system. TRAF the older papers for just fifteen extra minutes a day.

It may be a few weeks—or months, depending on the accumulation—before you begin to see your desk's surface, but the exhilaration produced by the steadily widening pool of clear space will serve as an exciting metaphor for the crisis of time you're averting as you take charge of more and more aspects of your life.

Wielding Your Time Management Tools

In the end, all we really have is *time*, and the choices we make concerning its allocation become the story of our lives. To achieve our goals we must learn to manage time. Two tools are essential, and I'll refer to them later in the book:

1. **The Master List**—this is your overall to-do list.
2. **The Daily List**—this is your everyday priority list.

These two simple lists, the Master List and the Daily List, will act as your blueprint for all the immediacies, as well as the long-term obligations.

The **Master List** is *one list* of everything you have to do, both big and small—self-generated or assigned by someone

My Master List	My Daily List
Schedule cat's shots	**#1**
Paint the storeroom	Outline weekly sales report
Joe and Jenny's 10th anniversary	Call to schedule mammogram
Begin diet—lose 15 pounds	Send flowers to Mrs. Morris
Quarterly report due soon	**#2**
Plant pansies & impatiens	Pick up dry cleaning
PTA—second Monday of month	Call Mom
Annual mammogram	Research for health report
Car inspection	Buy shoes for Molly
Pay quarterly taxes	Draft sales letter
	Call circulation for new stats
	#3
	Call vet for cat's appointment
	Hem slacks
	Organize party list
	Write birthday card to Aunt
	Susan

else, at home or at work. Jot a note in your Master List as soon as something comes up—your boss asks you to write a report, your gutters need cleaning, the cat's due for a checkup at the vet. The Master List is not a "working" To Do list. It might contain fifty or more items—far too many to keep track of on a daily basis.

One day after a seminar a woman who was a department head at the local power company came over to me with an anxious look on her face. She showed me her "to do" list, which numbered sixty items, and cried, "I can never get it all done!"

"Of course you can never get it all done," I reassured her. "No human being could ever accomplish this many tasks in a day or two. Without realizing it, you've created a Master List—a list of all your tasks from which you draw the actual tasks that you wish to accomplish each day."

Which brings us to the Daily List—a manageable list of actual tasks that you intend to accomplish on any given day.

Your **Daily List** is a short list of five to ten items that you intend to accomplish that day, divided into three levels of priority:

#1 Priorities: These are your *Absolutely Must Dos*. Never place more than two or three tasks on this priority level. Schedule your Absolutely Must Do priority tasks for the time of day you have the most focus and energy. Many people are at their peak in the morning, but there are others who start off more slowly and gain energy as the day progresses. If you're in the latter group, try to reserve your priority tasks for afternoon.

Gain time for your top priorities—hide out! Whether you close the door to your office, duck into an empty conference room, or find a solitary spot at home, make it clear that you're not available. You're in a meeting with yourself and can't be disturbed.

TEN THINGS YOU CAN DO WHILE YOU'RE ON THE PHONE

1. Clip items from newspapers or magazines
2. Review the next day's schedule
3. Organize your desk
4. Clean out a file
5. Mark items you need in a business catalog
6. Wash dishes
7. Address envelopes
8. Make out checks to pay your bills
9. Feed your cat
10. Walk on a treadmill

#2 Priorities: The second level of priority tasks are those that require medium effort on your part and have no urgent deadline. These are the basic substance of your day—doing research for an upcoming meeting, reviewing the budget figures, washing the car.

#3 Priorities: The lowest level of tasks are those that are routine and can be accomplished quite easily. Making an appointment, running an iron over a business shirt, TRAFing the incoming mail are things you do when you're a little bit tired. Priority 2 and 3 tasks are carried out "between the raindrops," as time permits, as compared to the more pressing Priority 1 activities for which you need to allocate a specific time.

Where should you keep your Master List? For many, low-tech works best. Write your Master List in an ordinary spiral-bound notebook. It should be big enough to write in, but small enough to carry with you wherever you go. It should always be at the ready to note tasks and assignments. Don't worry about organizing, prioritizing, or "izing" anything. Remember, it's simply the warehouse.

Some people prefer two Master List notebooks, one for work and the other for personal matters. Others prefer to concentrate all tasks into one notebook. Or use the same notebook for both work and personal tasks, but use a tab to separate them. Do whatever works best for you.

Those comfortable with the latest in high technology might prefer to store their Master List on one of the popular new handheld computers. I don't, however, recommend keeping your Master List on a computer, be it desktop, laptop, or handheld. It seems to me that if you wish to add to it at a moment's notice, a quick jot on a notebook Master List is preferable to booting up an electronic gizmo. It's a neo-Luddite viewpoint, I know, but pen and paper have their own pleasure.

QUICK PROBLEM SOLVER

SITUATION: "I need to keep up to the minute on industry reading, but I can't find the time. The journals are piling up."

SOLUTION: Check the table of contents of each journal, and tear out or copy only the top two or three articles of interest. Toss or pass on the rest of the magazine. Put the articles of interest in a folder to read while you're waiting for an appointment, stuck in traffic, traveling, or relaxing in the evening. Use the same technique with newspaper articles. To actually get through an article more quickly, one executive I know reads the first paragraph of a piece, the headlines, and the last paragraph, then skims the rest. Along the way, she jots down the two or three most important points in the margins.

SITUATION: "My husband and I commute by car for an hour and a half each day. Is there some way we can use this 'lost time' in a better way?"

SOLUTION: This is a great opportunity to catch up on reading. Have the passenger read aloud to the driver. Or listen to business or self-help tapes in an area of common interest.

Some couples use this time to go over personal business—such as planning their social calendar or talking about the kids' summer camp arrangements.

Why not use your commute time restoratively? Take turns driving and let the nondriver nap, read, or simply relax.

If you're commuting alone, books-on-tape or language tapes can be listened to while driving to and from work. Listening to tapes is even easier if you're using public transportation.

SITUATION: "I have a hard time getting off the phone with tele-marketing people. I don't want to be rude, but they take up so much of my time."

SOLUTION: Hey, they're invading your privacy. You aren't the rude one here. One woman's solution: She says, "I'm sure you don't want to waste time with me, when you might have more success with your next prospect—so, goodbye." Then she hangs up.

SITUATION: "What's the best way to keep the little things—gathering the newspapers for recycling, making doctor's and hair-dresser's appointments—from falling through the cracks? I know how to organize the big jobs, but those miscellaneous items always get put off."

SOLUTION: When I found myself in the same bind—lots of loose ends piling up—I created what I call "the daily fifteener." Every day I set the kitchen timer for fifteen minutes and do as many little jobs—polishing a pair of my favorite shoes, cleaning out my purse, making a dental appointment, ordering from a catalog—as I can accomplish in that period of time. It's truly amazing how many small tasks can be crossed off your list in fifteen minutes.

CHAPTER 2

Reviving the Family System

The Family That Works Together *Works*

My friend Martha is the office manager for her husband's dental clinic. She also coordinates her two daughters' school and social lives, as well as her household—cooking, cleaning, shopping, laundering, and organizing. This summer she's planning the family's move to a new house. Most weekends find her hip-deep in packing, making content lists for boxes, and shopping for the things they'll need for the move. Meanwhile, her husband is on the golf course, and her daughters are hanging out at the mall with their friends.

What's wrong with this picture?

Martha's family is loving and generally happy, but somehow it got established early on that Martha was the caretaker, and it became acceptable to turn a deaf ear to her occasional complaints and cries for help.

Being everyone's selfless slave is exhausting and unfair. It can also be isolating. Your family is over *there* doing whatever they want in their clean, comfortable home—the one you're responsible for providing—while you are still over *here* doing all the things that have to be done to keep everything running smoothly!

Why has Martha put up with this inequitable distribution

of labor for even one day? I suspect she got swayed by the soci-
etal messages that are aimed at women. A worthwhile woman
is praised and extolled as one who single-handedly takes care
of her family, one who *does* for her family—gives, sacrifices,
always goes out of her way to make a good home for them.

Has it been written that a worthwhile woman does all of
what seems to be required of her without help of any kind?
Naturally, modernity has created tremendously convenient and
time-saving devices—refrigerators and freezers, automatic

QUIZ: HOW COOPERATIVE IS YOUR FAMILY?

❑ Each person is assigned daily tasks.

❑ You don't feel as if it's up to you to do it all.

❑ You could be gone for a day or two without dire consequences.

❑ Your children understand that privileges and responsibilities go
hand in hand.

❑ You and your partner basically agree about who is responsible
for what tasks.

❑ You usually don't have to ask for help more than once.

❑ Your children have learned age-appropriate tasks as they've
grown.

❑ Family chores are completed in time for everyone to relax in the
evenings.

❑ You have an established time every week when the family talks
and plans together.

❑ If someone in the family can't do his or her tasks, the others
pitch in.

Score:

7–10: Your family works together.

4–6: A good start.

0–3: You need HELP—fast!

washers and dryers, dishwashers, stoves and microwave ovens, cellular phones, even sport utility vehicles geared to appeal to women. But even with all these conveniences at hand, it is still usually one woman contending with it all. Countless husbands still rely upon their wives completely for their every necessity, as do countless generations of children who look to Mom for everything—clothes, money, rides, meals, and love.

Today, with opportunities for women being abundant *outside* the home, many women, instead of being "liberated," now feel obligated to be almost superhuman. They feel compelled to try to successfully be all things to all people—mother, wife, partner, and full-time careerist.

Actually, until fairly recently the expected levels of cooperation within a family were radically different from the laissez-faire attitude that has sprung into being seemingly in just the last half of this century. Great-grandpa's tales of walking three miles to school in the snow *after* he had milked the cows and fed the chickens seemed like fairy tales, but the message was clear. Children were obligated, trained, conditioned, and expected to make a meaningful contribution to the family's well-being. Yet it appears that the children of the last two or three generations have been cheated of that very natural experience of doing their part. The family, in fact, is deprived of the very real services that each of its members can perform.

What happened? When did the experience of being part of a family in which every member shared some responsibility for the functioning of the household shift to a completely *different* paradigm of total childhood exemption from responsibility? When did the concept of complete entitlement become the norm?

Traditionally, a family has been a cooperative community, every member sharing some responsibility for the life of the household. But many parents today have a very hard time making any demands on their children. It's almost as if something *really* did get into their orange juice when they were kids. Perhaps in reaction to the strictures of their own childhoods, they've gone too far in the other direction. They believe that the role of a parent is to make sure the kids are happy all the time—that the children never be asked to perform tasks they dislike, that they never feel burdened by family responsibilities, that they never have too much stress placed on them. This misinterpretation of the parental role creates the opposite of what it hopes to achieve. Instead of instilling a sense of happy, grounded connection, an aura of familial cooperation, a sense of being a part of a unit and doing your part to make that unit function effectively, it creates chaos and discontent.

In fact, I saw a TV commercial recently that really chilled me. It was a cough syrup commercial that showed two little children trashing their house and screaming, with the parents looking on with sheepish "kids will be kids" smiles on their faces. Only when a child was felled by illness, and had to take the sponsor's cough syrup, did this couple exert parental authority.

It's sad that Madison Avenue has chosen an image of parenthood that reflects all too truly the realities that many families face. And frankly, I don't think family life lived that way can be much fun—not for the parents, and not for the children, either. Addressing this epidemic of childhood entitlement is urgently required, and a remedy needs to be instituted.

Consider a reordered life, filled with family cooperation. You might find more eagerness and less resistance to joining together in a family enterprise—a family co-op, so to speak—than you would ever have dreamed possible. Here are some practical ways of making the family a key contributor to your strength, energy, and well-being, instead of a drain on your time and resources.

First, let's play with the idea a little. What would an ideal home life look like for you? Let's say that you and your partner both work outside the home. When you walk through the door after a long day, what would you like to be greeted by? What if:

- The living room and family room were fairly neat.
- The children's rooms were reasonably neat and in shape.
- The laundry that you washed, dried, and folded last evening had been sorted and put away.
- The kitchen floor had been swept and mopped.
- The table had been set for dinner.
- The salad had been made, and a main course was heating in the oven.
- Phone messages were neatly arrayed under magnets on the fridge.

And, if you have teenagers who can drive, what if:

- Some of the grocery shopping had already been done.
- Dry cleaning had been picked up.

Does that seem like an impossible dream? It really isn't. All you need is a system.

Three Steps to a Family System

Even if you're coming to this late in the day, and your family life has taken on the quality of ships passing in the night, it's never too late to start pulling together the disparate pieces of your household. There are three primary steps.

Step 1: Develop a Detailed Task List

Before you do anything else, get clear in your own mind the scope of the tasks involved in running your household. Make your brainstorm as specific as possible. (If you use the Master

List system as described in chapter 1, your Master List note-book would be a handy repository for this task list.)

Divide your list into two categories: Daily and Weekly/Biweekly. Daily tasks would include items such as:

make the beds

transportation for the kids to and from school

wash the dishes

walk the dog

dry the dishes and put them away

peel and cut vegetables

feed the baby

Weekly/Biweekly tasks might be:

do the laundry

grocery shop

put gas in the car

change the bedsheets

vacuum the main living area

Step 2: Call a Family Meeting

Explain that you're going to be instituting a more cooperative system of family living. You might refer to it as a fairer system. Kids are sticklers for fairness—especially when they're the ben-eficiaries—and they'll understand the concept, whether they like it or not.

Ask each member of your family to go through the same exercise you did at the beginning—have them imagine how they'd like the house to look when they come home from work or school. How would they like it to feel? What would they like to count on having been done? What would make every-one's life easier?

While this is not supposed to be a forum for airing gripes, don't be surprised or terribly distressed if the family council evokes deeper issues: Do you have to be away so much? Why can't we come home from school to the smell of baking cookies? Why can't our friends come over and stay with us when you're not home? Why can't we be alone in the house?

It might twist your heart, but for now, write these complaints in your notebook, and table them for later examination. Incidentally, the family system is an important idea whether both parents work outside the home or not. An important goal—in addition to sharing the load—is to teach children to cooperate, share, and learn to take on a part of the responsibility, as well as understanding and appreciating the work of others that benefits them. At your family meeting, try not to get diverted by side issues. Don't avoid them. Just make a date for a separate meeting to discuss those issues.

Take out the list you've already compiled, and ask everyone to brainstorm additional items as they occur to them, until you have a fairly complete list. Take into consideration individual needs. Transporting Laurie to her weekly ballet class should go on the list, as well as buying supplies for Jeff's ongoing science project.

Step 3: Figure Out Who Does What and When

There are two ways to go about deciding how tasks are allocated, either of which can be successful depending on your family's style. The first method is one in which the chores that everyone does are relatively fixed. In other words, Jeff takes out the garbage, and Laurie has to help with vacuuming. The second method involves rotating jobs, so one week Jeff takes out the garbage, and the next week Laurie takes it out. The same rotation can apply to vacuuming, washing dishes, or any other routine chores. You might also choose a combination of the two methods.

Draw up two charts like the ones shown in the following

pages—one for daily tasks and one for weekly and biweekly tasks. Be sure to add a column for outside help.

I'm a big believer in delegating tasks outside the home whenever convenient. So, for example, picking the kids up from school could be worked out with a baby-sitter or a neighbor who also has children. I'll talk more about getting outside help in the next chapter.

Daily Tasks

1. Make a chart that looks something like the one shown on this page.

2. In the left-hand column, list the tasks that need to be done every day. Be as specific as possible. For example:
   set the table
   walk the dog
   transport the kids to and from school
   make the beds

DAILY TASKS

Tasks	Mom	Dad	Jeff	Laurie	Outside

wash the dishes
dry the dishes and put them away
peel and cut vegetables
feed the baby
take out the garbage

3. Now look at the names across the top. These represent all the members of your family, plus a category labeled outside help. Place a check mark next to the family member or outsider who currently performs this task.

4. Review the list again. This time, place an "x" next to the person or persons who could potentially perform this task.

Weekly and Biweekly Tasks

Draw up a second chart for weekly or biweekly tasks and follow the same procedure. It might include items like:
do the laundry
fold and put away clean clothes
grocery shop

WEEKLY AND BIWEEKLY TASKS

Tasks	Mom	Dad	Jeff	Laurie	Outside

clean the bathroom
rake the lawn
drop off and pick up the dry cleaning

At your family meeting, assign tasks to each member. Be careful that

- tasks are carefully balanced in terms of time and effort expended, so everyone feels he or she is being treated equitably.
- tasks are appropriate to the age and skills level of the child.

The Family Lottery: Make It a Game

Here's a more flexible way of allocating family chores that is actually a lot of fun—a family lottery! First assign each task a certain point value, depending on the time it takes, its desirability (for example, some may feel that folding laundry is a little higher on the desirability scale than taking out the garbage), and the effort involved.

Next, assign each person in the family a weekly number of "chore points" to earn.

Finally, to distribute the tasks, hold a weekly lottery. Here's how it works: Cut chips out of construction paper. Write the job's weekly point number on one side of the chip and the job itself on the other. For example, if vacuuming is considered a two-point "medium" task that needs to be done twice a week, assign the chip a point value of four. Once a week lay the chips out, with the numbered side facing up. Each person draws his or her assigned points without knowing what the jobs are. At week's end, the chips are returned to the "chip bowl" for another drawing. To prevent a small child from picking jobs that are too hard, put "little people" tasks on different-colored

CHILD-SIZED TASKS

Ages 2–3: Very young children enjoy playing at being little adults. They love using the dust buster, picking out items at the supermarket, putting their dirty clothes in the hamper, pairing socks, and separating light-colored clothing from dark. It's fun for them to imitate what you do.

Ages 4–6: As children grow older, they like to make a contribution that stretches their limits. For example, feeding the family pets, helping to prepare dinner, polishing the furniture, sorting books and toys, putting away the clean laundry, and making the baby laugh.

Ages 7–11: When children reach elementary-school level, they are proud of being old enough to make real contributions that stress their independence and your trust in them. For example, being sent to the market to pick up necessary items, learning to do the laundry, loading and emptying the dishwasher, writing down phone messages, planning the family menu, and learning to prepare simple dishes are all things they want to do.

Older kids: Yard work, shopping, errands, transportation, ironing, washing the car, cooking, baby-sitting. The cooperative spirit may pale with adolescence, but with a solid base, it should remain intact.

chips. Depending on your point system, each person might be responsible for between 15 to 20 points a week—maybe fewer for the younger members.

Clearly define the time of day when a child's jobs are to be completed—either before school, directly after school, or by dinnertime. Don't let these chores become bones of contention—make certain that they don't linger into the evening, when everyone is tired and tempers have grown shorter. These suggestions are not to be used as a new source of bickering material.

As to family clutter, sometimes stern measures are called for. Establish a family rule that clutter is not acceptable after twenty-four hours. One mother solved her clutter problem by stuffing stray items that were lying around into a laundry bag if her twenty-four-hour rule was broken. Family members had to apply to reclaim their possessions, and those who had been particularly lax—with a personal CD player, clothing, or a video game—might not get their things back for a day or two.

Whichever chore system you decide on, it's great to use your family meetings to work together to solve logistical problems. For example, "David has to study every minute for the next three weeks for his finals. What can we do to keep things going and take some of the pressure off of David?" David's

---

LOTTERY SYSTEM

Special Projects   4 Points
clean a closet
clean the basement
mow the lawn
wash the car
wash the windows

More Difficult Tasks   3 Points
scrub the bathroom
mop the floors
grocery shop
do the laundry

Medium Tasks   2 Points
cook a meal
vacuum
set the table
wash the dishes
change the bed sheets
feed the baby
walk the dog

Simple Tasks   1 Point
make the bed
pick up toys
take out the garbage
feed the cat

family, when faced with this exact situation, came up with the idea of trading points. His younger brother and sister would temporarily take over some of David's chores, and he would "pay them back" after his finals by assuming some of their jobs.

Making It Stick

Here's a basic rule of life: Kids forget, kids can be ornery, kids will by their nature as kids test the limits that you set for them. So don't get upset if, after an initial burst of enthusiasm, things begin to fall apart. Actually, this is a great opportunity to teach the kids about consequences—something they have to learn in order to get along in the world.

There are two kinds of consequences: natural and imposed. A natural consequence is something that just happens. For example, if a child leaves the milk on the counter instead of putting it back in the refrigerator, it will spoil and he won't have any for his morning cereal. An imposed consequence is one you create. This is more difficult, but necessary. From the get-go, kids need to understand that when a commitment is not kept, some kind of action will be taken. Make sure the consequence you impose is commensurate with the situation. You wouldn't say, for example, "You didn't vacuum, so you're grounded—for the rest of your life," although it may be tempting if a child is being obstinate.

There may be a certain amount of door slamming and sullenness, but when calmer seas prevail again, your child

> **GIFT IDEA**
>
> The next time your partner or children have a birthday, give them a coupon book with 10 to 20 points. This also makes a great stocking stuffer at Christmas.

may decide that it's worth his or her while to do better the next time. This process is one way we teach children to get along in the world.

On the other hand, be sure to show your appreciation when your children do their part. Positive reinforcement works, and sometimes a reward for special effort is a good idea—dinner out, a treat, a movie, and lots of hugs, kisses, and praise for a job well done.

One Family's System

A couple of years ago I was having an overnight visit with my cousin Michael, his wife, Jenny, and their two daughters— Karen, fourteen, and Roseanne, eleven. They invited me to stay in Karen's room while she slept over at a friend's house.

That was the most "up close and personal" view I've had of a fourteen-year-old girl's room for a while, and I must say I was surprised. Sure, there was plenty of young teenage froufrou: ruffly dolls and teddy bears, trinket boxes, photos of family and friends, books, CDs, posters, etc. But there was no "junk"—no boxes shoved into the back of the closet, no over-flowing shelves, nothing jammed into corners or spilling out onto the floor. Everything was clean and orderly.

The next morning I sneaked a glance into Roseanne's room and saw the same thing—plenty of kid stuff, but no mess. Again, her possessions had their places in a neat, orderly, and pleasant room.

I was quite surprised, because almost everywhere I go parents of children ranging from very young to the teenage years will lament their kids' rooms, which seem to range from relatively benign "pigsties" to positively dangerous fire hazards. The parents constantly harp on their kids to keep their rooms clean, but to no avail. So I just figured this was the way of the world.

I asked Jenny and Michael how they'd created this seemingly effortless order and organization in their children's lives,
and they had some very interesting things to say:

- From the beginning of their marriage, Jenny and Michael
  had always tried to equally share the load themselves.
  There was never an attitude in the household that one person should do everything.

- This was passed on rather easily to the girls when they
  were very young. Children learn by observing, so when
  Karen was just a toddler, and she saw Mommy and Daddy
  cleaning up together, she wanted to help. When Roseanne
  came along, she naturally wanted to imitate her big sister.

- Jenny and Michael actually *taught* their girls household
  skills. Jenny, for example, worked every day with the girls
  until they mastered bed making. And here's a great way to
  teach a four-year-old how to set a table: outline a table setting—plate, glass, cutlery, napkin—on a sheet of construction paper that the little one can use as a guide. Hours
  spent teaching? Quite a few. Hours saved when the kids
  know what to do? Hundreds. Value of skills for the children? Incalculable.

- Jenny devised a chart system for daily tasks, which she
  posted on the refrigerator. As tasks—like making the bed
  or putting away clothes—were completed, the girls would
  race into the kitchen to paste gold stars on the chart.

- Jenny and Michael are relatively relaxed people, and they
  avoided being too rigid. Some flexibility was built in so
  that the girls didn't feel as if they were in boot camp. For
  example, Jenny wasn't averse to saying, "Forget making
  the beds—let's go to the beach." Rather than making the

girls more lax, this flexibility gave them more motivation to do jobs that needed to be done.

Jenny, Michael, and their daughters represent some very hopeful and important models that all families who are seeking to "get out from under" can take heart from.

First, they are no throwback to the 1950s. On the contrary, their career situation mirrors that of many overstressed families today. Michael is an engineer with the government, and his work requires him to be away a good deal. Jenny is a computer expert who manages two forums on behalf of a large computer firm and has started her own computer consulting company, all while she completes her master's in an area of computer science. I get tired just thinking about it.

Jenny had the opportunity to work part-time when the girls were small, and then as they began to grow up, she began to take on greater work responsibilities.

But she made one very important point to me: "Michael and I have always made sure we all get together once a day for family dinner. That was and continues to be a sacrosanct, solid, 'core event,'" which she feels has had a great deal to do with maintaining their solidity as a family.

Organized Kids Make Life Easier

Although I'm sure the charm of having organized children won't have escaped you, it might not be clear to you how this connects with our overall theme of getting out from under.

Actually, it seems to me that to have organized children will have a real impact on your peace of mind on three levels:

The practical level. If your kids are organizing and cleaning up after themselves, then you're not!

The emotional/psychological level. So much of parenting stress is caused by the frustration of having to make the same demand again and again. The complaints, arguing, and nagging that a lack of cooperation engenders quickly grow old and become fruitless. If your children began moving to take charge of their own lives—at least at the minimal level of taking some responsibility and performing routine chores, such as straightening their rooms, wouldn't it lighten your emotional load?

The values level. In the end, organization is a tool toward the attainment of mastery and comfort in life. By putting this tool in your children's hands, you are giving them the gift of a lifetime—one that they will reap the benefits of over and over forever.

Okay, you're sold! Now comes the adventure, and I use the word advisedly, of helping your children become organized beings. How is this magic done?

Many people don't realize that organization is a learned skill, like reading and writing, that needs to be taught. It's not in your genes. Most people who have problems with organization just don't know how to do it!

If organization has been an issue for you, then teaching your child how to be organized will help you as well. The earlier you start, the more natural it will seem. Once learned, organizational skills will stay with your child for life.

Tips for Kids from Two to Twelve

Basically, organization for a young child centers around his or her room. Try these ideas:

Set up the room to foster organization. Nothing elaborate is required beyond putting hooks on the closet wall at a level a two-year-old can reach, putting a hamper in the bedroom for dirty clothes, and providing enough shelves to lay out the toys, books, and games—rather than jumble them up into a box or chest.

This idea of laying out toys and games individually is a technique favored at the Montessori schools. A friend of mine whose little boy went to a Montessori school explained that they place different-colored trays on shelves, and the children learn to categorize toys by color—blue tray for the blocks, yellow tray for the dolls, red tray for toy cars and trucks. Children find it easy, and even fun, to know where things go and to put them there.

Organize the room around the child. Here's the key: Fit the room to the child, not the child to the room. That means creating a flexible system that will "grow" as your child does. For example, even a very small child can hang up clothes if the closet bar is at the right height. Install a tension bar that you can adjust upward as your child gets taller, until he or she can manage the regular closet bar.

Also make sure your child can easily work the knobs to pull out drawers and open the closet. Place the hamper for dirty clothes in a corner of the bedroom to make it simple to dump clothes at the end of the day.

Categorize games and activities. Fundamentally, organization is about categorization—learning to identify categories and then to organize them physically. It's not that different from showing a child how to complete a puzzle. For example, one little girl was having difficulty with an Alice in Wonderland jigsaw puzzle. Her mother said, "Well, let's look at the picture on the box. See, Alice's apron is white. So let's first gather up all the white pieces and see if we can't put them together into the apron." When that was done, they went to the border pieces, and assembled those. Within an hour, the puzzle had been completed.

You can use a similar method to help your child learn categories for putting things away in his or her room. Make a game of it. Sprinkle various clothing items around the room, and play identifying the cubby or drawer that each item goes in—such as, "Can you find the shoe place? Where's the T-shirt bin?"

Four-year-olds can begin pairing their own socks together when they're ready to be sorted. They can do the same with their T-shirts and underwear, too.

Make a pleasant daily ritual out of organizing the child's room. Each day, as part of the bedtime ritual, help your child hang clothes on hooks, toss dirty clothes into the hamper, and choose clothes for the next day. One mother I know makes laying out clothes fun. She lets her three-year-old daughter arrange the clothes on the floor in the shape of a little girl. And they're ready to be put on in a flash the next morning.

Establish standards. By the time your kids are four or five years old, you'll need to have established some standards for what it means to "clean up your room." It isn't necessarily clear to them. As one boy told me when I was helping his family to get organized, "Mom yells at me to clean up my room, but I don't really know what I'm supposed to do. So I just push my stuff under the bed."

Make your standards clear and simple. You might try creating a checklist that looks something like this:

> Bed made
> Clean clothes put away
> Dirty clothes in the hamper
> Toys in the toy box
> Books on the shelf

And so on. The job always goes more smoothly when your child knows exactly what is expected.

Create incentives. The paths of organization don't always run smoothly. And let's face it, no child is going to say, "I can't wait to clean up my room!" Sometimes little Melissa or Robert will get ornery and announce, "I won't."

Without making a big deal out of it, let your child know that there will be consequences. For a small child that might mean no time for a story—since Mom has to pick up the clothes. For an older child, a reasonable consequence might be missing a favorite TV show.

On the other hand, when your child does a great job or makes a sincere effort, don't forget to praise him or her. An occasional reward is okay, too, as a way to express appreciation for a job well done.

Organizing Tips for Teens

After about twelve or so, it's a losing battle to try forcing a child to be organized. You need to pick your battles, so to speak, and maybe you don't want to spend your precious "capital of authority" on demanding a well-ordered room. However, it may be possible to make a deal.

Here's a successful scenario from one mother who made a deal with her fourteen-year-old daughter, Doreen. The word *organization* had never loomed very large in Doreen's vocabulary, and as a result she was constantly losing things and experiencing morning crises. She often couldn't locate her notebook, or the shoes she wanted to wear. Finally, Doreen's mother, Margaret, thought the time had come to try to release Doreen from the chaos in which she lived—a room stuffed to the gills with clothes, books, CDs, dolls, trinkets, magazines, and posters, with barely a clear path to the bed.

Margaret suggested a deal. She would work with Doreen over a period of time to reorganize her room, and as a reward at the end of the project, Doreen would receive a new desk and computer.

So, Doreen—not caring a fig for organization, but intrigued by the promise of a computer, which she desperately wanted—agreed. They set aside fifteen or twenty minutes a day, and began to tackle the job one stage at a time.

Stage 1: Clear out the existing debris

Doreen was, like many kids, a packrat, keeping everything she had ever worn, used, or played with. So working systematically around the room, starting with what was on the floor, taking one maybe three-foot-square patch at a time, Margaret picked up each item individually, and asked Doreen if she had used or worn it within the last six months.

The "no's" weren't discarded at this time—Doreen would have dug in her heels. But they were tossed into a "halfway house" carton. When a carton filled up, it was carried to a storage area in the basement, with the idea that it would be reopened in six months, at which time Doreen could keep whatever still had value to her. The rest would be given away.

The "yes's" were left in place, to be dealt with in Stage 2.

After the floor area had been sorted out into Yes and No piles, they pulled out whatever was under the bed, and then moved to the shelves, which were stuffed with books and toys and games dating from Doreen's infancy to the present time. So they chose fifteen toys that had special sentimental value, and put the rest in halfway house boxes.

Next they tackled the closets, then finally Doreen's drawers.

It turned out to be a big job! The whole clearing-out process took about three months, because they were working slowly. But two things happened unexpectedly as they went through the cleaning-out phase. First, Margaret and Doreen weren't fighting about what went into the halfway house boxes. The objective dividing line of use within the past six months made it easy to designate items—and Doreen knew she would have a chance to go through the boxes again. In fact, they spent a good deal of time laughing over some of the things their archaeological excavation uncovered. It turned out to be a nice time to be together.

Second, once Doreen got the hang of saying, "I do use or wear this," or "I don't use or wear that"—that is, making choices—she became much clearer in her own mind about what was valuable to her and what wasn't.

And as a totally unexpected benefit of this newfound ability to choose, Margaret noticed that Doreen was becoming more selective in other areas as well—such as how she spent her after-school time and the types of friends she hung out with.

Stage 2: Organizing the room for comfort and convenience

Now that the room was more "breathable," Doreen and Margaret set themselves to the actual organizing.

The first major task was to tackle the *closets*. All the stashes of Doreen's hangable clothes that had been kept during the clearing-out phase were brought to the closet and hung up. It was jammed. There just wasn't enough space. So Doreen and Margaret expanded Doreen's usable closet space by buying a plain metal hanging rack, the kind used in stores, and putting it in an alcove in Doreen's room. They hung a curtain over the alcove, which Doreen could close when her girlfriends were visiting.

Next, they took a look at *drawers and shelves*. Here, too, some expansion was needed, so they bought a set of interlocking plastic crates, and used them to hold the old toys Doreen had kept, as well as her impressive T-shirt collection.

Finally, they examined the *room itself* from the point of view of comfort and convenience and made some changes.

For example, to enter Doreen's room necessitated squeezing through a narrow passage between the wall and the bed.

Now that the room was clear of debris, there was space to move the bed and rearrange the furniture to make a more open and breathable room. Plus there was now a place for the new desk and computer. Doreen's dad, Doug, pitched in to help paint bookshelves and install curtain rods—and Doreen's room had been transformed—slowly, but transformed—into a space fit for the terrific young woman that she was.

Stage 3: A serious celebration

Just about the time the room organization was complete, Doreen's fifteenth birthday was coming up. So the family, who lived near New York City, had a combination birthday blow-out and organizing celebration, treating themselves and two of Doreen's best friends to a Broadway show and a night on the town. This was a serious expenditure—a Broadway show and dinner at a nice restaurant in New York City don't come cheaply.

But Doug and Margaret were so thrilled, not only at the organizational skills Doreen had gained, but at the increased maturity and greater responsibility she was assuming for her own life, that they were happy to mark the occasion in a special way.

The following week the computer arrived—and one more thing. While they were going through Doreen's old toys, Margaret had secretly retrieved an old Raggedy Ann doll that was in dire condition; the stuffing was spilling out, the hair in a tangle, the dress torn. Remembering how much Doreen had loved this doll when she was little, Margaret set about restoring it. As a surprise, she presented Doreen with a fixed-up Raggedy Ann, saying, "Here's an old friend for your new room." Doreen was so happy she burst into tears. When I heard this story, I was impressed once again with the many hidden values in getting organized.

Among Adults: Negotiation Is the Key

How about the adults in the house? Are you a pack rat and your spouse a mess? Does your roommate leave the dishes in the sink until they form colonies? Do you have college-age or adult children living at home but acting as if they've graduated from the need for family considerations?

There is one fact of life that cooperating adults need to accept as a reality: *You cannot force another adult to change. You can only negotiate satisfactory terms for compromise.*

When I work with couples who have different concepts of organization, I try to focus on the areas of potential compromise. You'd be surprised at how many "neatniks" get paired with "slobs." What may have seemed inconsequential before they lived together becomes a major conflict once they're sharing the same turf.

For example, Henry was a total slob in the bedroom he shared with his wife, Nancy. Having been brought up in a family where the boys considered it their mother's God-given duty to pick up after them, he didn't quite get it that times had changed.

So Henry would toss his clothing and wet towels around with abandon, and Nancy would pick up after him because she liked an orderly room—although she'd be fuming all the while.

Talks, discussions, arguments were all to no avail. Henry would try to stay neat for a couple of days after a blowup, but then his resolve would fail him, and he'd return to his previous habits.

Things were rapidly going downhill, when Nancy had a bright idea that satisfied both of them. They installed a floor-to-ceiling roll-up screen in one corner of the room, creating a small hidden area where Henry could deposit his stuff. This was a great solution: Nancy got her neat and orderly room, and Henry was able to be a slob in peace.

Once Henry had his private area, he found that dumping his dirty clothes and wet towels into his little space really wasn't all that pleasant. As a result, he got things a bit more under control—he actually began hanging his towels up after a shower, and started using an open hamper for his soiled clothing items.

Another couple worked out an equally creative and fair solution to the same problem—another husband whose consciousness hadn't been raised yet about putting away his own stuff. Ray and Ellen had gotten into the same constant hassles as Henry and Nancy. Their solution was to negotiate a trade.

Understanding that Ray would never in his lifetime satisfactorily pick up after himself, they made a deal. Ellen would take care of Ray's clothes, including sewing on buttons, getting clothes laundered and dry cleaned, sorted out, and folded. In exchange, Ray would take on complete responsibility for Ellen's car—filling it with gas and oil, washing it, getting tune-ups and inspections, making sure the tire pressure was correct, and handling the insurance and registration.

This suited them perfectly, and neither person felt put out by the other.

Pack-Ratism: What to Do with All the Stuff

A pack rat is not necessarily disorganized or sloppy. A pack rat is someone who keeps accumulating without ever disposing of anything.

Many people have trouble letting go of things—like the man I know who still has his electric bills from 1976, and the

---

YOU MAY BE A PACK RAT IF...

- your attic is crammed with boxes that you haven't opened for five years.
- you save every Christmas card—even the one from the local dry cleaner.
- any of the following items have been taking up space for more than six months: a lamp that needs a new shade; a picture frame that needs the glass replaced; an old typewriter you've been meaning to give to charity; an old chair you found on the street that you're planning to refinish.
- you have a shopping bag full of expired coupons.
- your high school prom dress (circa 1972) is still hanging in your closet.
- you have more than twenty coffee mugs.
- your stack of magazines dates back two years.
- you have a box of address labels from your previous home.

---

mother who has carried the idea of sentimental value to the point where she has saved every one of her son's eight hundred-plus drawings.

In one family who consulted me, it was the husband, Mark, who sighed and told me, "When I'm not using something or wearing something anymore, I just want to get rid of it. I hate feeling burdened by things I don't use any more. But Julie's just the opposite. She's still got her college notebooks, and there are all these boxes of her stuff stuck in the back of closets and under the bed."

I gave it to Mark straight: "Rule number one, you're not going to change Julie. Don't even try. For whatever reason—insecurity, sentimentality, possessiveness—she needs her stuff.

"Rule number two, you're not going to feel less oppressed

HONEY, I SHRUNK THE HOUSE

Here's an exercise to try if you just can't decide what you truly value and what is just taking up space in your life. Imagine that each room in your house was shrunk to half its size. For example, your 12'x16' living room is now 6'x8'. You can even draw a scale model. Now decide how you'll furnish the space with the things you already have—and what you'll need to get rid of.

---

as time goes on. You may adjust to it, but there'll still be a constant sense of stuffiness and unease."

At this point, Mark threw up his hands and exclaimed, "Thanks a lot for clarifying my impossible plight."

"Well," I said, "it's not as if you don't have options. You could move to your own, separate, immaculate space."

"Hey, we've only been married for three months," he protested.

"Or," I continued, "you could make sure that Julie has a space for all of her stuff." At this point, I put him out of his misery and offered the following ideas:

1. If space permitted, they could clear out an underused room and line it with industrial shelving for Julie's stuff, leaving aisles to walk through.

2. They could erect a small, secure prefabricated shed in the backyard. (In the house where Mark grew up, for example, his father had a little backyard shed where gardening tools and old business records were stored.)

3. They could rent space in a warehouse facility for approximately $40 a month. Many facilities have as much or as little space as one might require, ranging from small storage lockers to cavernous rooms.

Mark realized that the storage facility would be the logical answer. He didn't relish the expense, but wryly admitted, "Let's just say it's what I'll do for love."

QUICK PROBLEM SOLVER

SITUATION: "I'm a part-time parent and only have my kids every other weekend. Our arrangements are pretty makeshift, but I still want the kids to feel as if this is their home, too. Is there a family system that works for part-time parents?"

SOLUTION: "Makeshift" is a state of mind. Every lifestyle can have a system imposed to make things run more smoothly. Begin by realizing that there is no such thing as a part-time parent. You are actually a full-time parent with part-time caretaking responsibilities. The goal is to make your time together as normal—i.e., structured—as possible. Hold a family council with your kids, and spell out a routine and a set of expectations. Establish a space for the kids' things. Even if it's a shelf, toy box and a few drawers, require that they take care of keeping it neat. If possible, purchase duplicates of key items to reduce the amount of lugging back and forth, and packing and unpacking—which only reinforces the feeling that your kids are visitors. Prepare meals at home, and put a limit on the takeout and restaurant dining. Most important, try to put aside your personal differences with your ex-spouse, and be allies when it comes to child raising.

SITUATION: "I'm moving into an apartment with two friends and we're going to share expenses. I've never had a roommate before. What would you advise?"

SOLUTION: Before you so much as stick your toe in the doorway, establish a common understanding and a set of house rules. Put it in writing. How many people have discovered after the fact that their roommate has a fondness for loud music at 3:00 A.M., or a habit of forgetting to pay the phone bill, or a tendency to have friends dropping in at all hours? Once you're living in a situation, it's very difficult to set rules. A key to success is to make sure that each person has a space that allows complete privacy.

SITUATION: "It takes me twice as much time and effort to get my six-year-old to help with the chores. I have to supervise him and often do it over again. Since my goal is to save time, wouldn't it be easier to just do it myself?"

SOLUTION: It might be easier in the short term, but think of your efforts as an investment in a lighter load later. If you impress upon a child from an early age that he is a participant in the family system, it will become natural for him to help out. To make things easier now, lighten your standards. Everything doesn't have to be done perfectly. And look for simple tasks that he can perform on his own—such as straightening up his room or separating colors from whites in the wash.

CHAPTER 3

Co-oping, Bartering, and Buying Time

The Joy of Outside Help

My friend Julie, a wife and mother with a full-time job at an advertising agency, agrees that the whole family should pitch in to keep things running. And she plans to start getting her little daughter Charmaine to help out almost as soon as she can stand on her own two feet—Charmaine is six months old. However, Julie is adamant about not hiring outside help. She can't explain it really. Fundamentally, she just thinks it's more responsible to keep family business in the family. "We chose this lifestyle," she reasons. "We wanted to have a child. It doesn't seem right to dump it all on someone else. Besides, if I'm going to be a working mom, I'd better learn how to juggle."

If I were a psychologist, which I'm not, I'd probably have a whole convoluted explanation about why people—and especially women—feel that they have to do everything themselves. I will say, however, that part of the problem is a chronic, anxious perfectionism: "I should be able to do it all—prepare lunches for school, do a couple of loads of laundry, get in a couple of neurosurgeries and rounds before being home by 3 P.M. I'll shop for dinner on the way home from the hospital, pick up the kids from their ballet and karate classes, and then prepare a delicious, balanced meal while waiting for my busy executive husband to appear at 5:24 P.M.—and I'll do it all beautifully to boot!"

This fantasy of perfection—of doing it all—is epidemic in our culture. It may have something to do with the extraordinary iconic power of Martha Stewart. Or perhaps it's an offshoot from the idea that men and women alike have more opportunities today than they ever did before.

Somehow, in the last few decades, the idea emerged that what you do has more value if you do it yourself. Asking for help—even if you pay for it—is a sign of weakness or inadequacy. The physical isolation created by suburban sprawl has brought with it a psychic isolation. It's harder to view those around us as part of a cooperative community, and we cringe when we have to ask even our closest friends to lend us a hand.

What would it take to restore the community concept among friends and neighbors—to become less isolated and consider ways we can share the load?

The Art of Co-oping

A quiet movement that is spreading across the country involves groups of people—neighbors, friends, acquaintances—pooling their time, skills, and resources to cooperate in daily life. Co-ops can be organized around just about any need. Here are a few suggestions:

1. **Child Care Co-op.** Start a baby-sitting co-op with friends and family members. Use a point system to keep track—for example: 2 points per child per hour, 1 point per child per meal. Assign one person to schedule and coordinate the baby-sitting. This co-op works best for families whose baby-sitting needs are roughly the same. (For additional advice, the National Network for Child Care has published

a set of guidelines for starting a baby-sitting co-op. Information is available from the Extension Distribution Center at Iowa State University, 515-294-5247.)

2. **Skill Sharing Co-op.** Trade a skill that you have for a service you need. For example, exchange computer lessons, housekeeping, child care, or cooking for meals, lodging, transportation, child care, or elder care.

3. **Barn-Raising Co-op.** Organize a neighborhood fix-it group. Just like in the good old days when people got together to raise a barn, gather neighbors and friends for projects like painting a house, installing storm windows, landscaping, hauling trash, and building fences.

4. **Cooking Co-op.** You can make this work with three or four other families who can agree on basic menus and budgets. One or two days a week, you cook and deliver dinner; the remaining days, dinner is delivered to you.

5. **Bulk Food Co-op.** Stores that sell food in bulk are becoming common everywhere. If you'd like to take advantage of the savings without having to keep a mammoth freezer and pantry, organize a group of family, friends, and neighbors to share a membership in one person's name. Rotate the weekly shopping chore. The purchaser can arrange to drop orders off individually or bring everything home to be picked up by the members.

6. **Hand-Me-Down Co-op.** If your attic is cluttered with baby and toddler clothes, high chairs, and toys that your children have outgrown, you're not alone. Consider starting a club with other parents to recycle these items. You might produce a monthly notice pairing what's available with items people are looking for.

7. **Friends in Need Co-op.** Organize a neighborhood help service that comes to the aid of a family in need—for example, cooking meals and running errands for a neighbor whose husband is in the hospital, or pitching in to help a new mother.

Case History: "Mom's Night Off"

Almost every night after work, Barbara, a financial services manager at a local bank, had to stop at the market. Often she ran into her next-door neighbor, Marilyn, a school librarian. One night, standing in line at the checkout, Barbara glanced into Marilyn's basket and joked, "Chicken again? Me, too. We might as well be shopping and cooking for one family."

The two women looked at each other and a light bulb went off. Suddenly, it seemed ludicrous that both of them were trudging to the same market, night after night, then returning home to stand at their stoves only fifty yards away from each other while they cooked practically the same fare for their families.

They decided to try an experiment; they called it "Mom's Night Off." One night a week Barbara would deliver a fully cooked meal to Marilyn's family (Marilyn, her husband, Bob, and their twelve-year-old, Sam), and one night a week Marilyn would deliver a fully cooked meal to Barbara's family (Barbara, her husband, Kevin, and their two children—five-year-old Emily and eight-year-old Samantha). So each woman, on her night to cook, was preparing dinner for seven people.

They set some ground rules. The meals would include a complete dinner—meat or fish, starch, and vegetable—but no dessert. Since neither family had a special diet, the menus would be open-ended within general nutritional guidelines. Best of all, no money would change hands. Each of them would pay for what she served.

The experiment was so successful that Barbara started talking about it at the bank. One of her co-workers, Jennifer, a single mother with two children, asked if she could join—and the dinner cooperative was launched. With the addition of an older couple on the block, they had four families, and twelve people. Dinners were exchanged Monday through Thursday, meaning each family had to cook only one meal during the workweek.

To keep things simple, the co-op emphasized meals that were easy to prepare for larger groups of people, and could be made in advance on the weekend or the night before—casseroles, stews, pasta dishes, and salads.

In the year and a half the dinner co-op has been operating, its members have realized two unexpected bonuses. "We started doing this for convenience," Barbara said. "It would have been benefit enough not to have to cook every night. But we're all surprised at how much money we're saving. Half or more of our weekly food budgets. For my family, cooking one big meal for twelve is much cheaper than cooking four meals for three."

The other benefit has been the bond that has grown among the four families. "When you share food every week, whether you're actually eating it in the same room or not, there is a primal connection," Marilyn noted. "We're a real community. I'm delighted my children are getting an opportunity to experience this."

Making a Co-op Work

What elements are needed for a truly successful cooperative effort? Let's take as an example a baby-sitting co-op and examine the six criteria for success.

1. A Common Understanding

The very nature of a cooperative implies commonality—meaning that its members need to share the same basic values and goals. For a baby-sitting co-op, it's of course vital that the adults feel comfortable with one another and trust that their children will be given satisfactory care. This is basic common sense.

2. A Common Need

A successful co-op brings together people whose needs are similar. A baby-sitting co-op, to work successfully, wouldn't combine kids who needed full-time day care with kids who required baby-sitting only once or twice a week, nor would it mix infants with older children. The more in sync everyone's needs are, the more smoothly your co-op will operate.

3. A Limited Membership

Most co-ops start with people who already know each other and feel comfortable together, but inevitably they grow. Open membership just doesn't work—and it's best to limit the membership at the start to a set number of families. When you're dealing with child care, you're probably going to want to be especially selective, and keep the group manageable so that everyone knows one another.

4. A Clearly Defined Commitment

Fairness in spreading the load is the nuts and bolts of a cooperative effort. If some members do all the taking and others do all the giving, the cooperative is not a cooperative—it's a service. From the outset, a minimum commitment must be established. Many co-ops find that a point system works best. In a baby-sitting co-op, each member would be responsible for a certain number of "points" every week. A point system might be something like this:

3 points per child under three years old per hour
2 points per child over three years old per hour
1 point per child for a meal

1 point per child per hour before 8:00 A.M. or after
9:00 P.M.

And so on. The point system will vary among co-ops.

5. An Organization

A successful co-op should have at least one person—perhaps on a rotating basis—who serves as coordinator and secretary. This person can be paid in points, although that may not even be necessary if everyone in the co-op takes a turn. The secretary keeps track of points earned and spent and gives a regular accounting. There should also be regular co-op meetings—a minimum of four times a year—to discuss how things are going and to handle any problems that may arise.

6. General Rules

If the values and needs of your members are relatively in sync, there won't be any need for a great many rules. You should nevertheless make certain to clarify some basic standards. For example, in a baby-sitting co-op, minimum standards might include:

- Special requests—someone may need a hand, be ill, or late from work.
- Sick children—how will sick children be handled? What about contagious diseases and basic sanitation?
- Emergencies—is a system in place to deal with any sudden problems that could occur—an injury, an accident, a sudden illness?
- Transportation—is there a reliable way to make sure children get back and forth from the co-op safely?

Case History: A Successful Food Co-op

Jacksonville Natural Foods is a pre-order buying club located in Jacksonville, Illinois. Every four weeks members place an order, which is delivered the following week on a refrigerated truck. Members of the club come, unload the truck, split the delivery into individual orders, double-check the division, pay for their orders, and then take their food home. Any member who can't work on a delivery but has an order coming in pays a surcharge. The surcharges of nonworking members underwrite the expenses of the group—such as bank charges, computer costs, and telephone fees. Although one member is responsible for the ordering and invoicing at Jacksonville, there are various other arrangements that could work more equitably. For example, members could rotate the ordering and invoicing chores; or one or two members could take over the entire task and charge a small fee to members.

The Rebirth of Bartering

It wasn't that long ago when money as we know it—paper bills and coins—didn't even exist. Commerce was direct: two chickens in exchange for three bags of flour and a barrel of tomatoes. In fact, the first Roman coins were stamped with the image of a cow and backed by cattle.

Today, bartering has come back in a big way. Bartering has experienced a renaissance as a common way of doing business. As a sign of the times, business barter resulted in the equivalent of more than $7.5 billion in sales in 1995, according to the International Reciprocal Trade Association, whose members swap everything from travel packages to printing services.

So, what can you swap? When we were kids, swapping was a way of life—my peanut butter sandwich for your bologna, Willie Mays for Mickey Mantle. It was fun because it gave us access to things we wanted but didn't have or couldn't afford. My sisters and I used to swap toys, clothes, and chores. It was especially gratifying when you walked away thinking you got the better deal.

HOW TO START YOUR OWN
SERVICES EXCHANGE

Here's how three creative women living in a large Chicago apartment building created a services exchange that now has thirty members.

1. They began by sending a letter to every apartment, introducing themselves and outlining the concept of the exchange. The letter contained a form listing examples of services that could be exchanged—for example, shopping, cleaning, hairdressing, cooking, computer lessons, laundry, typing, baby-sitting, car care, driving, painting, repairs, dog walking, piano lessons, sewing, and résumé writing.

2. A week later, they followed up by knocking on doors and speaking to interested residents. They spent time helping people brainstorm the types of services they could offer and what they themselves needed. The initial response was enthusiastic but cautious. This was a large building, and people didn't know each other that well.

3. Once the ice was broken, the organizers realized they needed to hold an event that would catalyze the exchange and allow people to get to know each other. They hosted a potluck cocktail party in the building's common area, and more than fifty people attended—including several who hadn't initially been interested. Each person wore a name tag printed with a service he or she could offer and one he or she needed, for example: "My name is Carol Grassley. I give computer lessons. I need transportation." The party was a huge success, with lots of on-the-spot swapping.

Two years later, the services exchange is still going strong. In fact, a building association has been formed to coordinate the swaps. The best part of all: the formerly isolated apartment dwellers are now a community.

For more information about how you can start your own barter
system or neighborhood exchange, a great resource is
Co-op America, 1612 K Street NW, Suite 600, Washington, DC
20006; 800-584-7336.

To orient yourself to the mindset of bartering, sit down
with a notebook and brainstorm what you could offer. There
are three main areas of barter—skills, resources, and time.

Skills

• Do you have professional skills, such as accounting, typing, construction, sewing, writing, fitness training, catering,
etc., that you would be willing and able to use for barter?
Obviously, some skills are easier to trade than others. Also
keep in mind that a business exchange of services might have
legal or tax consequences. The IRS may consider certain
barter—the exchange of professional skills, for instance—as
valid as exchanges of cash, making it taxable. Also, even if
you're bartering a service, you're making a contract, so bartering may legally validate a responsibility, and make you legally
responsible for any negative outcome of your bartered service.

• Do you have abilities that come naturally to you or that
grew out of hobbies, such as playing an instrument, photogra-
phy, crocheting, baking, gift wrapping, gardening, fashion
sense, etc., that constitute services people often pay for?

Resources

• Do you have resources that others might share, such as a
car you use for commuting that has room for more people,
yard tools and equipment that could be traded, computer or
electronic equipment to be lent, a spare room that could be
used as a work space, a pickup truck that might be lent for

hauling, and so on? Make a mental inventory and write down your resources.

• Also include possessions you have that are in good condition but that you no longer want or need, such as furniture, appliances, clothing, equipment, or books.

Time

• If you have time, that may be the most valuable commodity of all. What time-saving services could you offer? For example, dog walking, house sitting, personal shopping, waiting for repairmen, shuttling kids, picking up medicine for the ill or elderly, even waiting in line to pay a bill or get a registration renewed.

Once you begin making a list, you may be surprised by how much you have to offer. The next question is, How do you find a match? Read the sidebar "How to Start Your Own Services Exchange" to see how one group did it.

Buying Time

The refrain "Time is money" certainly holds true for many overextended people. However, I continually encounter an astonishing reluctance to pay for reasonably inexpensive services that may in the long run reap tremendous benefits in terms of quality of life. I think this gets back to the guilt trip we discussed earlier—the feeling that "I should be able to do it myself."

Instead, think of *functions* that other people could handle for you. A freelance journalist friend has hired young people whom she euphemistically refers to as her "elves" ("little people who run around a lot"). Through the placement offices of two local high schools, she keeps a group of five or six students working. One elf does typing, another checks references at the

---

QUICK PROBLEM SOLVER

SITUATION: "When I'm hiring household help, how can I guarantee that I choose the right person?"

SOLUTION: The first rule of thumb is to avoid making hiring decisions when you're desperate. If you need a baby-sitter in three days, a seamstress tomorrow, and a caterer by the weekend, you'll be more likely to make a quick decision that could cost you later in aggravation—and worse. Here are some tips to avoid mishaps:

1. Be clear about your expectations. If you want your cleaning person to do windows, don't keep it a secret. Write down a job description for anyone you hire.

2. Before answering an ad or calling a service, ask your friends and co-workers if they can recommend someone. Personal referrals are usually best.

3. Thoroughly check references—even if someone has been recommended by a friend. Your standards may be different.

---

library or on-line, a third supervises two of my friend's younger children.

Today it's possible to receive services in your home that you once had to go out for—often for little or no extra cost. Some examples are services from a veterinarian, manicurist, tutor, exercise trainer, accountant, lawyer, and auto mechanic.

There are also many companies that provide free services to accommodate the increasingly busy two-career family. For example, your local dry cleaner may offer free pickup and delivery, and the supermarket may take orders by fax or over the phone and deliver your groceries at no extra cost. And here's a tip: If a store in your area doesn't already offer a service you

4. Trust your instincts. If during the interview you have an uncomfortable feeling, but can't pinpoint it, go with your gut.

SITUATION: "I'm one of those 'sandwich generation' women that people are always talking about. I have two young children plus a semi-invalid mother at home. Is there help for me?"

SOLUTION: Many people are in your situation these days. Happily, there are an increasing number of home care services available. Check out your state or local agencies for the aging, and ask your doctor or clergy to recommend agencies. Depending on your mother's condition, many services may be available, including visiting nurses, therapists, "friendly visitors," meals-on-wheels, personal care providers, drivers, telephone checkers, and support services that will give you time off from caretaking. You can also order a free copy of "How to Choose a Home Care Provider" by sending a self-addressed stamped envelope to the Consumer Guide, P.O. Box 15241, Washington, DC 20003.

need, ask the manager. Chances are he or she will be willing to accommodate you in order to keep you as a satisfied customer.

I firmly believe that the *most* time-saving and worthwhile service is having someone run your errands. Hiring a reliable student or a retired person to do the marketing or make pickups and deliveries creates a real shift in time. When you think of it, it's so often all those "life maintenance" chores that consume an hour here or a half hour there that eat up so much of our weekends. Wouldn't it be more satisfying to spend those precious hours with our families or just relaxing?

CHAPTER 4

Taking Time Out

Don't Forget to Give Yourself a Break

Have you ever known someone who—no matter how large her apartment or house, her purse or her suitcase—always manages to fill it up? One of my clients, Claudia, was like that—except her modus operandi was to be a *time* filler, not a space filler.

After I spent six months helping Claudia get organized, work more efficiently, and take advantage of outside help, I was baffled that she seemed to be just as harried as she'd been at the start of our work. It turned out that Claudia just couldn't stand having free time. As soon as she freed up an hour, she found some other way to fill it. I found out that Claudia had been raised in a very strict household, where the motto was "Idle hands are the devil's workshop." That explained her aversion to relaxation. Changing her tune was another matter. It required that Claudia start viewing "free" time as "planned relaxation" time—and consider it every bit as important as any other appointment.

If you're like Claudia (and many overworked people are), here's some food for thought: You are not the Energizer Bunny! If you try to keep going and going without recharging your resources, you'll run out of juice.

It's sometimes hard to grasp the reality that overachievement can be a form of self-sabotage. All of the efficiencies, organizational strategies, and support systems we've discussed in the first three chapters are virtually meaningless if you can't learn to think of time taken for yourself—a well-deserved time-out—as time well spent.

Small Breaks That Make a Big Difference

Here is a little known fact: Frequent small breaks during the course of a day can be as refreshing as long time-outs. Think of these mini time-outs as energy rechargers, as pressure valves for an otherwise hectic life. You can interweave brief physical and mental time-outs into your day, simply by making them an

---

QUIZ: ARE YOU READY TO RELAX?

Take this quiz to find out your level of resistance to relaxation. You may have unconsciously conditioned yourself to always be mentally and/or physically edgy.

1. When you take a vacation, do you leave phone numbers where you can be reached?

2. Do you often find that you don't have time to exercise?

3. Do you find that doing nothing drives you crazy? For example, do you have to have a magazine or book to read, or notes to write, if you're forced to wait five minutes for an appointment?

4. Have you ever pretended to be busy so other people wouldn't think you were slacking?

5. Is personal time your lowest priority?

If you answered yes to any of these questions, your ability to relax may be too low. Make an effort to take time off.

integral part of your normal flow. The key to this process rests in discovering the opportunities that already exist in your day for five-to-fifteen-minute breaks. Here are some ideas:

1. **Morning Routine.** If you're up and running as soon as your feet hit the floor in the morning, rethink your routine. The manner in which you start your morning can have a tremendous impact on your stress levels for the remainder of the day. How about rising ten minutes earlier so you can relax with your coffee or have time for some stretching and breathing exercises?

2. **Commuting.** If you commute to work by car, play calming music or listen to a book on tape during your drive. If you take the train, use headphones.

3. **Hourly Breaks.** Get in the habit of "taking off" for three minutes of every hour. A writer I know gets up from her desk at three minutes to the hour, every hour, to stretch her legs and walk outside to her garden. She finds that these tiny breaks are tremendously restorative.

4. **Eye Closers.** Close your office door and close your eyes for ten minutes in the middle of the day. Many people find that the hour after lunch is their lowest energy point, and a ten-minute catnap is usually a tremendous relaxant and energizer for the afternoon ahead. Perhaps that's why so many cultures include a "heat of the midday sun" siesta as a part of the daily rhythm of their lives.

5. **Activity Break.** Exercise is known to reduce stress, lift depression, and increase energy. Close your office door and stretch. Go into the stairwell of your building and walk up and down the stairs for ten minutes—five minutes down, five minutes up. That will get your heart pounding. Take a ten-minute walk during your lunch break.

6. **After-Work Time-Outs.** If you have children and you work outside the home, those first few moments after you walk in the door at night can be sheer madness. Establish a time-out rule that Mom or Dad won't be available for fifteen minutes, and take time to change your clothes, wind down, and make a mental transition before you face the family.

7. **Shut Off the Noise.** Leave the TV off for a night or two every week. One of the best ways to relax is to limit the stimuli—radio, TV, CDs—that have made the outside world too much a part of our intimate lives.

8. **Alternate Mental and Physical Activities.** If your job requires heavy mental concentration, use your off time to perform activities that are more physical—and vice versa.

9. **Small Pleasures.** Read for pleasure at least fifteen minutes a day.

10. **Do Nothing.** And sometimes, the best relaxation method is to do absolutely nothing at all.

Relax by Moving

If the pressures of daily life leave you so exhausted and frazzled that all you can think about is collapsing into bed, try this instead: Get up and go. Many studies show that certain forms of physical exercise improve your mood, reduce your stress levels, and give you added energy. One reason is that exercise increases the concentration of norepinephrine, a neurotransmitter responsible for emotions and stress responses. Some experts also believe that physical exercise "conditions" our bodies to physiologically adapt to stress.

Most of the successful executives I have worked with over the years considered exercise essential; I rarely encounter one who claims to be just too busy. These men and women have figured out that exercise is a secret weapon in their work.

Here are a few tips:

- Choose an activity you enjoy and that is convenient. How many health club membership cards gather dust in drawers because people don't like the environment, are bored by the classes, or find the location too inconvenient? A twenty-minute walk around your neighborhood that you look forward to beats a workout at the health club you never get to.

- Consistency is more important than intensity. A business executive I know decided to take up racquetball because he figured it would give him the best workout. It also gave him the most injuries. Between a sprained ankle one month and a bruised hand the next, he got very little exercise. So although you may enjoy an occasional game of touch football or other physically intense sports, you might be better off with a more reliable activity.

- Enlist a buddy. If you're having trouble getting started, you might feel more motivated if you have a companion. Cora, the busy dean of a community college, was determined to start exercising, but with all the other things she had on her plate, she couldn't get started. Finally, she asked a friend if she would join her three days a week for an early morning walk around the local lake (about two miles). Having company was the perfect solution for Cora. The two women walked and chatted, and neither of them minded the workout.

Be Sure to Schedule Time Out

If, like most busy people, you have difficulty viewing time out as time well spent, force yourself to change your attitude. Write it on your calendar—or on the priority portion of your Daily List. Your thirty minutes for gardening or twenty minutes for yoga should be listed right along with your important meetings and errands. I know a woman who works at home who has achieved the shift in attitude. She isn't afraid to let people see the big bold letters on her desk calendar:

1:30 P.M. NAP

PART II

Examine Your Personal Universe

CHAPTER 5

The Solar System Technique
Finding Out What Really Matters

If some of the organizing ideas in the previous chapters have proved to be of value to you, then the chances are you've been able to convert some of them into concrete changes that provide some breathing room in your busy life—small oases of relative calm. And, frankly, that may be all you need. As someone once said to me, "You know, I *love* my life. I don't really want it to be any different. I just want to live more comfortably and spaciously *within* my life. It's not as if an outside person would notice any changes—but *I* would notice. And so would my family."

But for other people, a remarkable thing happens on the way to getting organized. It wakes them up, reminds them of thoughts they'd buried. They've cleared the trees just enough to see the forest. All they can see, for mile after mile, is *more trees*. The idea of continuing to trudge along the path of an endless forest, ultimately going nowhere, seems intolerable. If someone were to say to them, "For the next ten or fifteen years, you're going to basically have the life you're living now," their response would be utter dismay.

If you believe that you fall into this category—or somewhere in between—perhaps it's time to sit down and identify your values. What gives you satisfaction and pleasure? I don't mean the satisfaction of a hot shower, a good day at your job, a delicious meal. I refer instead to what really matters—the basic values that form our lives—family, relationships, work, interests, faith, aspirations, and home. How many people today are so dedicated to one aspect of their lives—their careers, for instance—that other, equally important parts of their lives are for the most part ignored? An assessment of values always threatens to unleash a torrent of self-rebuke, because values aren't just a list of ideas or feelings. They translate into tangible, legitimate needs and desires that require action, and trying to meet those needs and desires can leave you feeling overwhelmed, helpless, and guilt-ridden.

What level of pressure do you feel within yourself as a result of your conflicting values? The collision of shifting standards, as well as greater expectations surrounding quality-of-life issues, has created ever higher levels of stress and anxiety in nearly everyone's day-to-day existence.

It may sound heretical, but perhaps people have developed too *great* a level of expectation and demand in their lives. Is it possible that a person can actually have *too many* values instead of too few? I think so. Maybe you've set the bar of your life impossibly high.

For example, would it be all that unusual for a typical man or woman to state that all of the following activities represent important values to him or her?

- being involved in all staff meetings at work
- spending quality time every day with the family
- checking on the status of any reports he or she is responsible for presenting, several times during the week
- staying in the office during lunch and catching up on any urgent matters
- keeping up to date on professional journals, and filing the helpful articles

- exercising at the gym three times a week
- scheduling regular meetings with all subordinates to make sure that all projects are under way
- clearing, compiling, and filing all pertinent office materials—papers, e-mail, faxes, and memos

All of these activities have varying levels of importance, but if a man or woman were to give equal weight to all of them, he or she would probably have to give up sleeping. Life would be a mad dash! It would be impossible to give completely focused attention to so many tasks, so ultimately he or she would feel the pressure of all of the other *shoulds*:

> "I *should* have worked out twice this week. I have to try to do better."
> "I *should* have made it to little Julia's dance recital!"
> "I'm a lousy friend. I *should*'ve called Kevin weeks ago."
> "I *should* cancel dinner with Martha so I can finish this report for work."

And the constant inner wail: *What kind of mother am I? What kind of father am I? What kind of person am I? What kind of son-daughter-husband am I?* It goes on and on, a catalog of reproach. Why? Because you've set totally unrealistic goals for yourself.

This is where the Solar System Technique comes in. If you feel you need to get started on some major changes, the Solar System Technique will let you shape your personal universe into a concrete visual pattern. By that I do *not* mean visualization, meditation, journal writing, or any of the other rather ambiguous exercises you may have tried before. The Solar System Technique measures your actual, nitty-gritty reality. It is ultimately a highly refined organizational strategy that will help you progress from a person who *talks* about change to a person who *activates* change.

The Solar System Technique

The Solar System Technique has nothing to do with astrology, and everything to do with real life. As you'll see, the solar system provides an excellent metaphor for helping to establish the relative values of everything from home to work to religion to family. And the key to the Solar System Technique is the way it enables you to ask yourself important questions about your own life.

I have always been fascinated with the way that asking the right question in the right manner can evoke a revealing reply, resonant with meaning. This is the genius of good interviewers, such as Larry King and Barbara Walters. Good interviewers have intuitive skills that allow them to probe beneath the surface and pull out genuinely thoughtful and considered replies from people. That's what the Solar System Technique is all about. It is a method of conducting what amounts to a skilled interview of yourself—bringing to the surface what really matters to you, and then to break those values down into specific goals and tasks to help you bring your *real* life and your *ideal* life more closely into congruence.

For some time, I had been grappling with the issue of how to help my clients get to the essentials—to pull their deepest thoughts clear of the day-to-day static that tends to drown them out. The Solar System Technique began to take shape after a conversation with my close friend Sandra. Sandra is primarily a homemaker, with a part-time job as an interior designer for a furniture store. She told me that she and her husband, Ed, were browsing one day at a local farmer's market and she was rhapsodizing over how fresh the piled ears of corn looked. Ed looked at her quizzically and asked, "Have you ever thought of growing a vegetable garden?"

"Well, actually, no," she answered. "My father had a little

veggie garden when I was growing up and I sometimes helped him weed it. But I wasn't ever really involved in it. And after that, growing a vegetable garden never occurred to me."

But Ed's question stayed with her, and Sandra realized that it had touched some deep chord. She began to wonder why the idea of a vegetable garden was so persistent. Maybe there was a connection to her father, now deceased—the fond memories of her father delighting in his plump tomatoes and crisp cucumbers, the tug of regret that she hadn't spent more time with him when he was alive.

As Sandra thought more about the garden, she also saw a link between the garden and her profession. Interior design and growing a garden both reflected an intense sense of place—a connection to the land. She realized that her life's passion was about creating comfort and pleasure out of space—both her own and those of her clients. Unfortunately, her busy schedule of shuttling her kids from here to there and creating interior designs for other people's homes had left her little time to concentrate on her own. So she began to set aside small blocks of time to increase the beauty of her home, inside and out. And yes, she did plant a garden—flowers, not vegetables. The vegetables at the market were just fine, thank you.

Meanwhile, as part of her home improvement project, Sandra started taking some additional courses in design, and she found that she had a real interest in—and aptitude for—landscape design. She set about improving her knowledge and skills in that area, preparing for the day when her children were grown and she could pursue her career more fully.

Imagine! All of this from a fresh pile of corn—and Ed asking a simple question. I was fascinated by the power of that moment in the farmer's market. Sandra's experience showed me that if people were able to ask the right questions of themselves, they could find out what really mattered.

This method would be very different from all the other types of long-term goal setting that I'd seen. Usually, such methods begin with the statement of a general goal—for example, "I want to help people," "I want to make a lot of money," "I want to be an astronaut." With the goal as a starting point, they then break it down into all the practical steps that will, in theory, take a person to his or her goal.

The problem with this approach is that, for many people, those broad dreams seem too abstract and too far away. They often have little relationship to the realities of their daily life. Taking the first step can feel as hazardous as walking off a cliff.

The Solar System Technique takes you in exactly the opposite direction. Rather than starting out with the big picture, this method asks you to look first at the *details* of your life and organize them into what I call a *constellation of meaning*.

In this chapter, I will introduce you to the Solar System Technique, and walk you through it. We will begin with specific questions—similar to Sandra's vegetable garden question. Then we will move on to themes—as Sandra did when she began to see that her passion involved a sense of place and home.

In the next chapter we'll turn to the very practical matter of how to translate these wishes and desires into the achievement of goals: what you can do *right now,* and changes you can make to create a more content life a year from now, five years from now, and over the long haul.

Part III will show you how to turn those goals into the reality of personal change in the areas of work, family, finances, and the lifestyle of getting and staying out from under.

Setting Up Your Personal Solar System

We live in a solar system that consists of nine planets orbiting the sun. These planets range in distance from the sun, with Mercury being the nearest, and Pluto being the farthest. In the

Solar System Technique, the planets and their relationship to the sun form the *visual metaphor* for what has the most—and the least—meaning in your life.

As the illustration on pages 86 and 87 shows, each planet is located in an orbit according to its relative distance from the sun. The Solar System Chart is one of your primary work tools. The technique involves working through a series of statements and placing the code number of each statement where it belongs on the Solar System Chart in relation to its importance in your life. (You will find blank charts at the back of the book that you can photocopy.)

Now imagine that you inhabit your own personal solar system. You are the sun, at the white-hot center of your universe. The planets held within the power of your gravitational pull represent the vital principles that compose your life. In this exercise, I'm going to ask you to imagine that the things you love and hate are like planets in your personal solar system—and it's up to you to decide where to place them in the following orbits:

The Sun: At heart's core.

Is there an area that is of white-hot importance—blazing directly at the core of your being? Each of us has one or two things that are so important, so central to our lives and our sense of who we are, that they belong in the sun itself. For many men and women, being a parent is at heart's core. Some people would place their religious beliefs at heart's core.

Orbit #1: Of red-hot importance.

Is there something of burning importance that, like the planet Mercury, belongs very close to the sun? For example, some people might find that having an outlet for their creativity, or home schooling their children, falls in this category. A little far-

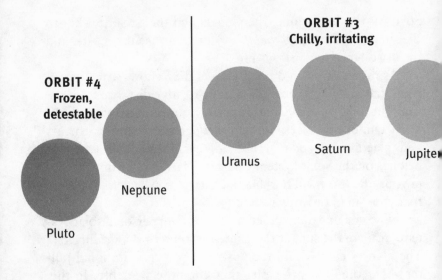

ORBIT #3
Chilly, irritating

ORBIT #4
Frozen,
detestable

Neptune

Uranus

Saturn

Jupiter

Pluto

SOLAR SYSTEM CHART #1

This highly schematic drawing of our solar system shows the order of the planets by their distance from the sun—from hot Mercury, to warm Earth ("third rock from the sun"), out to frozen Pluto.

Mark your personal solar system choices on a copy of the chart in relation to their distance from your *own* sun. (See pages 96 and 97 for an illustration of a chart that has been partially filled out.)

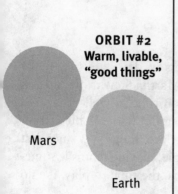

ORBIT #2
Warm, livable,
"good things"

Mars

Earth

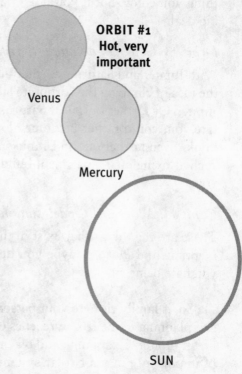

ORBIT #1
Hot, very
important

Venus

Mercury

SUN

ther away, but still of great importance, are Venus-like categories—perhaps being active in politics or spending time with friends.

Orbit #2: Of very warm importance.

The Earth elements are those aspects of daily life that make you content—the "good things," as Martha Stewart would say. For example, a baby-sitter who is on time, a well-organized office, a weekly book club meeting, a daily jog. A bit farther out are Mars-like elements. These are the things you enjoy but can take or leave. Perhaps, for example, playing tennis is something you enjoy, but if you don't have the time to play, it's no big deal.

Orbit #3: Chilly; of no interest; irritating.

With Jupiter and Saturn, we enter into a negative area. Perhaps the idea of climbing the corporate ladder leaves you cold—near Jupiter. Or farther out, near Saturn, most social occasions irritate you; you'd rather be home alone, curled up with a good book. Even farther out, in Uranus, may be a stronger dislike—such as living in an apartment building with people all around you.

Orbit #4: Active dislike, detestation.

These are the things that exist in the barren nether regions of Neptune and Pluto. Maybe you despise your current job, or you hate being single.

So, is family close to your personal sun? Is career? Is financial planning in the frozen reaches of outer space? Is your love life in Jupiter? Examining and placing these categories in order of importance in your solar system are tremendously helpful when attempting to gauge the value of the flurry of activities that compose your life.

It is important to enter the negatives as well as the positives. And if an item simply doesn't register—that is, you're completely indifferent to it or it is irrelevant—ignore it and move on.

The Basic Phases

The Solar System Technique will lead you through four phases:

Phase 1: Creating a snapshot of your present life.
Phase 2: Taking a deeper look to identify your ideal life.
Phase 3: Focusing on your priorities.
Phase 4: Identifying your life themes.

> **YOU WILL NEED:**
>
> • Several blank copies of the Solar System Chart
> • Pen or pencil
> • Notebook or journal to write in

For these exercises, you'll be using the schematic drawing of the solar system, with the sun at the center and the nine planets placed roughly in the order of their distance from the sun. Our solar system consists of nine recognized planets, and so I have identified nine basic arenas that are germane to our lives:

Family   Activities/Interests
Home   Friends/Community
Work   Health/Fitness
Spiritual/Philosophical   Financial
Intellectual/Cultural

Gather all your tools and find a space that allows plenty of elbow room. Let's get started.

Phase 1: Creating a Snapshot of Your Present Life

The purpose of Phase 1 is to give you a general picture of the way your life is now and how you feel about it. You won't be lingering over it at this point. Just be objective. Begin by taking

one blank copy of the Solar System Chart and labeling it
"Snapshot of My Life."

1. In your notebook, under each category listed on the previous page, write two or three simple, declarative statements
that characterize your life right now. Assign each statement a
code, using the first letter of the category (F for Family, H for
home, etc.), and number them in order. For example, in the
Family category you might put:

> F-1. I am married.
> F-2. My mother-in-law lives two blocks away.
> F-3. I have two children.

Under the Spiritual/Philosophical category, you might put:

> S-1. I attend church every week.
> S-2. I am interested in eastern religious practices.

And so on. Fill in each of the nine lists.

2. On your Solar System Chart, enter the codes for each
item in the appropriate place. For example, if next to F-1 you
wrote "I am married," and you view your marriage as central
to your life, place F-1 inside the Sun. If your marriage is in a
more ambiguous or negative state, you might place F-1 elsewhere on the chart.

Your mother-in-law lives two blocks away? For one person, this may be just dandy: Your mother-in-law is great with
the kids, you go shopping together, you've developed a real
friendship. So you might place the code close to Mercury. On
the other hand, maybe you dream about the day when you can
place more distance between you and your mother-in-law. In
that case, the F-2 code may fall somewhere around Saturn or
Uranus.

Often, where you are right now might be fine for the present, but you hope for something different in the future. For

example, in the Home category, you might have written, "Frank and I live in a two-bedroom condo." Someday, you'd like to live in a large, older house on a tree-lined street, but for now, you're happy in your bright, spacious condo. So place the code near the Earth, or even closer to Mercury, but in your notebook write down that this will change in the future. (Actually, there are many areas of life that are like that; just because you want something different later, doesn't mean you aren't content now.)

After you enter all of your "Snapshot" codes on the Solar System Chart, set it aside for the time being and move on to Phase 2.

Phase 2: Taking a Deeper Look to Identify Your Ideal Life

For this phase you will need to refer to the lists starting on page 108. (You will find a second copy of these lists in the Solar System Worksheet section at the back of the book for ease in photocopying.) You'll also need a second blank copy of the Solar System Chart. This is your primary working tool. You might want to label it "What Really Matters."

In each of the nine lists I've placed ten very concrete, very specific, actions or preferences that represent a range of choices. For example, under the Work category, "I like working on my own" is listed as item W-2. The lists aren't necessarily comprehensive; they're designed to cover general territory. You may add as many items as you like.

Go slowly through the lists, turning each item over carefully in your mind before placing it on the Solar System Chart. Don't worry about whether your placement is exactly right. This is a guide to yourself. There may be items that you're not sure about. Fine. Just approximate the placement on the chart. You can always change it later, when you begin working on the charts in Phase 3 and Phase 4.

You'll find that some statements are completely irrelevant to you. Just cross them out or ignore them.

Feel free to modify the statements or make them more specific. You can also add and delete items.

Sample: Melissa's Solar System Chart

Before starting work on your own charts, take a look at Melissa's Solar System Chart (see pages 96–97)—an example of the Solar System Technique in action. Melissa is a customer service manager for one of the "Baby Bell" phone companies. She is married to Gary, a brand manager for a large corporation. They live in Omaha, Nebraska, and have no children.

Let's walk through several items on the Solar System lists with Melissa, and watch how she decides where to place them.

FAMILY

F-1. I want to be married.
Melissa *was* married, and no doubt about it, her relationship with Gary was the most important thing in her life. So that was an easy call—inside the sun.

F-2. I want a child.
The statement about wanting a child brought an important conflict to the surface. (This, by the way, is part of the usefulness of the Solar System Technique: It gives you a dispassionate way to examine conflicts that you've pushed under the rug.)

Melissa definitely wanted a child. However, she believed strongly that a young child should have a parent at home, and Melissa loved her work. It was a major conflict—not to mention the financial strains she and Gary would face without her salary.

So Melissa entered F-2 in Orbit #1 because it was extremely important to her, and she placed an asterisk next to it and made a note in her journal that there was a conflict, so she could later explore this unresolved issue.

F-4. I'd like to be a stay-at-home parent.
Melissa knew that she wanted to be a stay-at-home parent when she *did* decide to have children, so she marked F-4 in Orbit #1, inside Mercury.

HOME

H-1. I'd like to live in an older house that I can restore myself.
Restoring an older house just wasn't on Melissa's radar screen, so she didn't place this item at all.

H-2. It's important that I have plenty of space.
Melissa thought having a spacious living environment was "a good thing," so she entered H-2 in Orbit #2, at the Earth.

H-3. I want to live in a city.
Live in a city? No thanks. Melissa had visited Chicago numerous times for business meetings, and she had been to New York City twice. She had enjoyed her visits to both cities, but she was very glad to get back home to more peaceful surroundings. So she placed H-3 in Orbit #3, out by Saturn.

WORK

W-1. I want to be fully absorbed in my work.
Melissa *was* fully absorbed in her work helping customers solve problems, and she enjoyed it no end. So she placed W-1 in Orbit #1, near Mercury.

W-2. I like working on my own.
Melissa knew she would hate working on her own. In fact, the very thing she loved so much about her job was that it allowed her to work closely with others. She placed W-2 in outer space, inside Neptune.

W-3. I like working in a small group.
The actual wording of this statement didn't really speak to Melissa's circumstances, so she crossed it out and wrote a dif-

ferent, yet related statement: "I like helping people out. It's important to me to be in a direct service or assistance capacity."

Well, this was surprising. Although Melissa had known that she enjoyed helping people, she'd never given it a lot of real thought. But her response to her revised statement was so powerful that she put W-3 inside the sun. She made a note in her journal. Clearly, service wasn't just a preference, it was a life theme.

As you can see by observing Melissa go through the process, the Solar System Technique can quickly evoke a deep level of awareness about what really matters to you.

Now it's your turn! Take your "What Really Matters" chart and start working through the lists that begin on page 108.

Once you've placed all the items that apply to you on the Solar System Chart, you may find that the exercise has triggered other inquiries—subcategories that you would like to explore. If that is the case, take a third blank chart and brainstorm your own subcategories.

For example, Donald was a young lawyer who worked as an associate in an old-line law firm in Boston. He had been thrilled to get his plum job, but now that he'd been at it for a year, he was very unhappy. In a word, the job was *boring*. Now Donald was very confused. It would be insane to give up a job that other young lawyers would give their eyeteeth for. And yet . . .

I suggested to Donald that he create a subcategory under Work, called Lawyer (code L), and begin listing statements that might apply to lawyering, in as objective a manner as possible. That is, I didn't want him to make judgments yet; the list should include items he might love as well as items he might not love. For example:

L-1. I want to do research.
L-2. I like to write briefs.

L-3. I want to work actively with clients.

L-4. I want to be an advocate.

L-5. I want to be a partner.

Donald created ten items, and as he began placing his Lawyer list items on the Solar System Chart, it quickly became clear that being an advocate and working with people held pride of place in his sun and in his Mercury orbit. He enjoyed the intellectual aspects well enough; doing research and writing briefs were interesting—but maybe for an hour or so a day, not *ten* hours. And the money-making aspects of making partner in a large firm (which he once had found so thrilling) had drifted out near Pluto.

Just at this time, Donald learned that his law school was looking for a recent graduate to pull together programs encouraging college undergrads to attend the school. This would entail meeting with students from all over the country (people), drawing up a defense of the school and the benefits it offered (intellectual), and figuring out what it would take to help students realize their full potential at the school (intellectual and advocacy). Donald applied for and won the job. Although he took a severe cut in pay, he found the job perfect for this point in his life.

Under Activities/Interests, Nancy put the statement "I need to have pets" right near the sun. This interest was so important to her that she created a subcategory called Pets. When she came to the item "I want to protect strays," bingo! That was it—right at the center. After that, Nancy became active in an organization that works with strays, and now she boards strays in her home until they can be adopted. It has added an entirely new dimension of pleasure and satisfaction to her life. In your search for what really matters in your life, you may also find yourself spinning off of one list or another into fresh arenas.

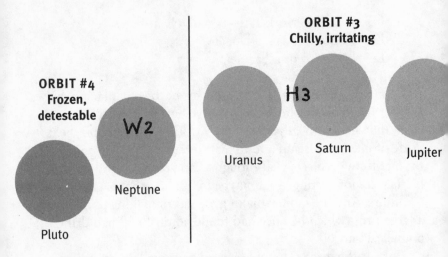

MELISSA'S SOLAR SYSTEM CHART

As Melissa worked through her choices and
entered them on her Solar System Chart, this is
how her chart looked.

If any of the categories triggers similar responses to those
that Donald and Nancy experienced, go ahead and create a
subcategory.

Actually, the Solar System Technique is infinitely expand-
able. You can take any item and expand it into a subcategory
to better define what you really want.

Take cars. We all know that cars mean different things to
different people. For some, a car is a signature—an extension
of identity. For others, a car is just a means to get from one
place to another. If you are about to buy a car, it might be fun
to explore what it represents for you. A subcategory, Cars,
might include statements like these:

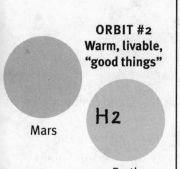

ORBIT #2
Warm, livable,
"good things"

Mars

H2

Earth

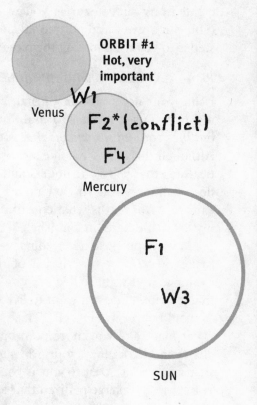

ORBIT #1
Hot, very
important

Venus

W1

F2*(conflict)

F4

Mercury

F1

W3

SUN

C-1. I want a Jeep or a Suburban.
C-2. I've always dreamed of owning a BMW.
C-3. I want the safest car on the road.
C-4. I see myself as a Jag person.
C-5. I don't care what kind of car I drive, as long
     as it gets me to work on time.
C-6. I will drive only an American car.

You could do a similar exercise with clothing and fashion, education, travel, or any other area.

After you have placed all the items on your chart, and have created any subcategories you want to include immediately (you can always add additional subcategories later), the next step is to begin evaluating the picture.

Phase 3: Focusing on Your Priorities

Using your notebook or journal, begin to organize the statements you used in Phase 1 and Phase 2. *I'd like you to write out the group of statements that you have placed in each orbit.* Although this may seem like a chore, it is actually a very practical step that helps you understand your choices. And it can be deeply illuminating to view them in groups. At a glance, you can see, "Ah, that is what constitutes my sun," or, "These are my loves and hates in a nutshell."

For the purpose here, you can rephrase the statements to make them more descriptive of their meaning to you. For example, if "I want to live in a city" is sitting out in Pluto, you might write, "I do not want to live in a city"; or, going further, "I would never live in a city." (See sample list on next page.)

It may take you more than one sitting to complete your charts and to organize your orbits into lists. Don't be surprised that revelations occur to you as you are working. For example, you may never have realized that seemingly separate facets of your life had anything in common until you saw them listed together in the same orbit. Emily, for example, was surprised that her love of skydiving was related to her profession as an emergency room nurse. Both involved an adrenaline rush of being in a life-or-death situation and having to make it work.

Phase 4: Identifying Your Life Themes

It can be a real adventure to tease out life themes that until now you weren't aware of. All of us have certain themes that form the guiding principles of our lives. Often, however, we are unaware of them. For example, the lawyer, Donald, discovered

(PHASE 1) SNAPSHOT OF MY LIFE	(PHASE 2) WHAT REALLY MATTERS
Sun (heart's core) I am a pediatrician.	**Sun (heart's core)** I want to be married. I want a child. I want my own medical practice.
Orbit # 1 Mercury (very hot) I interact with many people on the job.	
	Orbit # 1 Mercury (very hot) I need to be close to my friends.
Orbit # 2 Earth (warm, good things) I live in the city. I walk in the park every morning.	
	Orbit # 2 Earth (warm, good things) I want to live in the city.
Orbit # 3 Saturn (chilly, irritating) I am single. I work long hours. I work in a hospital.	
	Orbit # 3 Saturn (chilly, irritating) I dislike being single.
Orbit # 4 Pluto (detestable) I have little time to myself. I have little time to get together with my friends.	**Orbit # 4 Pluto (detestable)** I would never want to live in an old house in the country.

that a guiding theme for him was to spend his days with other people. That's where he found his strength. In fact, Donald mused, he may have been a successful law student at least partly due to the custom in his school of forming study groups that continued for the duration of law school. This collegial environment brought out Donald's intellectual strengths and allowed him to shine. He didn't think he would have done nearly as well on his own.

The following is a list of themes, or guiding principles, that are commonly found in people's lives. You may think of others:

LIFE THEMES
Adventure
Ambition
Art, music, literature
Beauty (person, home, possessions, environment)
Collegiality
Faith, religion, spirituality
Family
Figuring things out, problem solving
Financial security (or risk taking)
Health, fitness
Home and household environment
Independence, personal freedom
Intellectual pursuits
Invention, innovation
Leadership, managing others
Love, intimacy
Making a contribution, service to others
Nature
Parenting
Physical movement (dance, sports, fitness)
Power
Privacy, solitude

Risk-taking
Security
Status, standing in the community
Variety and diversity (people, environment, activities)
Wealth

Now, study your orbit lists. Are any of these themes (or others that aren't listed) reflected in the statements you have placed in your Sun and Mercury categories?

Write down in your notebook two or three primary themes that your orbit lists reveal.

For example, in connection with the first theme on the list, Adventure, I remember reading when Jacqueline Onassis died that her children remarked that a sense of adventure was one of her strongest characteristics.

Well, she certainly had an adventurous life! Not only did she choose a way of life that placed her constantly on the edge, but she was physically daring as well. Mrs. Onassis was an accomplished equestrienne, whose skills included jumping.

You might also respond to the theme of Adventure, but it might have an entirely different meaning for you. For example, Margaret worked for CARE in Africa in large part because she enjoyed the adventure of exploring unfamiliar cultures. (She also noted that flying a puddle-jumper from Somalia to Nairobi was an adventure that she *didn't* relish.)

Once you isolate a theme or themes, make a list under each of them to specify what that theme means to you. For example:

SPIRITUALITY
daily meditation
writing in a journal
creating *Feng Shui* in your home
playing chants in the background while you work
volunteering at a homeless shelter

Next, consider whether there are any apparent conflicts in your Solar System Chart. Is there, for example, a strong pull toward both work and home, or a desire for a large family but a need to live in an urban environment? Does one theme seem stronger than another? Explore that theme alone, and see if you can fit the values of your conflicting theme inside it.

For example, Frances, a packager of corporate meetings and conventions, noticed that there were two seemingly contradictory themes on her Solar System Chart—one of "security" and one of "freedom." This went a long way to explain why she was constantly bouncing from job to job. When she worked for an events packaging firm, she felt too constricted— frustrated with the politics and unhappy with the rigidity. But whenever she tried to be independent and sell her abilities on a freelance basis, she worried constantly about money and benefits and the future.

Frances began with the value of independence, and listed all the items that it included:

"Freedom to make my own schedule."
"Ability to use my creativity without being told what to do."
"No involvement in corporate politics."

Was there a place for "security" in this theme? That depended on what Frances meant by security. She realized that she wasn't interested in making a fortune—just enough compensation to live comfortably, and have benefits for health and retirement. Within that framework, there was a possibility that she had never considered: becoming a full-time independent consultant for one particular company, with an annual renewable contract and eligibility for the company's benefit package. To date, Frances is still working on a proposal, and admittedly it won't be easy. But she has taken the first step by clarifying her possibilities.

Here is another consideration. Do your hot value orbits seem very crowded? That may be a tip-off that you haven't yet truly defined what's most important and may need to go back and pinpoint your preferences more specifically. In my consulting business, I often run across this overload of priorities. I tell my clients, "Everything can't be a top priority. Think of it this way: The building is on fire and you have to get out. Now, *that's* a top priority! Learn to be more selective about what really matters. Begin with the question 'Do I need this in my life to survive—physically, emotionally, intellectually, spiritually?'"

On the other hand, you may see that you have very few items that are close to the sun. This might indicate that you have yet to discover your passion. Or perhaps you are simply a balanced, even-tempered person, who operates best at equilibrium.

You May Want More, Not Less

When we think about getting out from under, most of us assume that means becoming less pressured, and that's usually the case. However, sometimes satisfying your "soul spot" can mean becoming more rather than less engaged.

Take Rosalie. Rosalie is a divorced woman in her fifties, with grown children who no longer live at home. For about seven years, Rosalie spent most of her time looking after her increasingly frail parents.

After they died within a year of each other, Rosalie was left with a too-large house and a great deal of empty time on her hands. Prospects were bleak.

Rosalie began volunteering for odd jobs at her church, just to stay busy. Gradually she became more and more active with an inter-church agency that worked with homeless women; her involvement grew to the point where she joined the board. Then, two years later, Rosalie became executive director of the agency.

Now Rosalie's phone never stops ringing, her calendar is

booked full, staff and volunteers clamor for her time—and Rosalie has officially joined the ranks of the frazzled. And she couldn't be happier being there.

Doing the Solar System Technique Together

If you have a significant other, hopefully you're in the same orbits. I recommend that couples begin by doing the Solar System Technique individually, then putting the two charts together. The following method basically shows your level of compatibility. Clearly, compatibility is not such a cut-and-dried thing. Many people coexist happily in relationships with partners who have different interests and goals. And, of course, every relationship involves some compromise and give-and-take. On the other hand, if you are at odds regarding issues that are absolutely core to your being, you have issues that need to be addressed. For example, how many couples have discovered after they've tied the knot that one person desperately wants children and the other person doesn't? It happens all the time—not necessarily because people hide their true feelings, but more often because they haven't asked the hard questions about what each person wants and needs and tried to work them through. I have often felt that the ideal would be for every couple to do the Solar System Technique together before they get married.

Kate and Jerry: Different Orbits

Kate and Jerry ran into a barrier after they had been married only six months. They had always been aware that their social temperaments were different. Kate was extremely outgoing, had a big extended family and many friends. Jerry was a more private person who considered his home a sanctuary. Before they were married Kate and Jerry lived in separate apartments, and Kate's sociability rarely invaded Jerry's space. Neither of them stopped to consider what would happen when they lived together. When Kate's friends started dropping by to visit, and the phone rang constantly, Jerry felt as if an essential privacy was being destroyed. Three months into their marriage, Kate's brother, who lived across the country, came for a long visit, and the newlyweds had their first big fight. Kate's point: "This is my home. I should be able to have my friends and family here." Jerry's point: "Can't a guy even have peace in his own home?"

This couple never grasped the fundamental nature of their differences. A closer look at their priorities could have saved them a lot of pain in their marriage.

Couples Exercise

After you have individually charted your solar systems, do the following exercise together:

1. Compare your individual "hot" lists—that is, those items that appear in the Sun or in Orbit #1. On a separate sheet of paper, write the items—if any—that you have in common.

2. Compare your individual "cold" lists—that is, those items that appear in Orbit #4. On a separate sheet of paper, write the items—if any—that you have in common. Your two common lists might look something like this:

OUR HOT LIST
1. We want a large family.
2. Financial security is very important to us.
3. We want to be active in the community.

OUR COLD LIST
1. Travel is not important.
2. We don't need a lot of space.

3. It's not important to live near family.
4. We don't want pets.

3. Evaluate the results. Are there any items on your hot lists that you do not share? If so, is that a conflict? For example, if one of you feels passionately about having a dog, and the other person doesn't have strong feelings one way or another, it's not a conflict. However, if one person puts the dog on a hot list, and the other person is phobic and puts the dog on a cold list, there may be a conflict you'll need to work through.

Repeat the process with your cold lists. Remember, the cold list should include those things that you passionately do *not* want. Again, disagreements here aren't necessarily conflicts, but they can be.

When I have worked on the Solar System Technique with couples, a frequent question comes up: "What if we don't share any items on the truly hot or truly cold lists?"

I have found that some people are quite content to go along with their partner's passions. My friend Mark is an extremely mellow guy. He just doesn't get too worked up about anything. Valerie, his wife, is a bundle of nerves and energy. She's involved in every political protest, picket line, and fund drive that comes along. Mark enjoys Valerie's gregarious, intense personality, while Valerie finds Mark's easygoing nature a real port in the storm. Their differences work for them.

There is no rigid definition of compatibility. Even seemingly insurmountable contradictions—such as wanting to live in different cities, or having opposite political views—can sometimes make a match. Remember James Carville and Mary Matalin, political operatives who became well known to the public during the 1992 presidential campaign? Both were fiercely loyal, outspoken campaigners who generated plenty of heat and debate—he on behalf of Bill Clinton and she on behalf of George Bush. However, they made no secret of the fact that they were dating, and after the election they married and now have two children. These two give the impression of loving a good fight; time and marriage haven't changed that. I suspect that their household is a fairly noisy place. But at the core, they have found a way to be in sync.

If I may play the devil's advocate for a moment, let me also say that the old adage "opposites attract" may be true, but the chemistry isn't always good enough to endure the realities of life. If you're a die-hard loner and your mate happily welcomes neighbors and friends into your home at all hours of the day and night, perhaps your orbits are too distant. It depends on how much you're willing to work together to find a compromise that you can both feel satisfied with.

The next step of the Solar System Technique is matching the ideals in your solar system with your actual life, and bringing them into congruence. This is where you'll begin ironing out the rough spots and achieving some balance in your life.

SOLAR SYSTEM CHART

FAMILY

F-1. I want to be married.

F-2. I want a child.

F-3. I want a large family.

F-4. I'd like to be a stay-at-home parent, at least until my kids are older.

F-5. It's important that my spouse be extremely involved in family life, and not let his/her work take preference.

F-6. I'd like my spouse to be the primary stay-at-home parent.

F-7. I want to balance a full-time job with child rearing from the start.

F-8. My spouse and I should share the same religion and views.

F-9. I want to live in the same city as my parents and siblings.

F-10. I prefer to stay single.

HOME

H-1. I'd like to live in an older house that I can restore myself.

H-2. It's important that I have plenty of space.

H-3. I want to live in a city.

H-4. I want to grow my own herb garden.

H-5. I prefer small-town living.

H-6. It's important that I live very close to where I work.

H-7. I'd like a big yard.

H-8. I want to live in an apartment, with little or no upkeep.

H-9. I want a large kitchen.

H-10. I'd like to live in a community where I know my neighbors.

WORK

W-1. I want to be fully absorbed in my work.

W-2. I like working on my own.

W-3. I like working in a small group.

W-4. I want to work in a large company, with lots of options.

W-5. I'd like to be a manager and direct others.

W-6. I love generating new business.

W-7. I want a career that allows plenty of time for family.

W-8. I want to work at home.

W-9. I'd like a job that involves travel.

W-10. I want to own my own company.

SPIRITUAL/PHILOSOPHICAL

S-1. My religious affiliation is central to my life.

S-2. I consider myself a spiritual person, but do not practice a traditional religious observance.

S-3. I attend church or synagogue only on holidays.

S-4. I admire the spiritual wisdom of people like Deepak Chopra.

S-5. I want my children to be raised in a traditional religious framework.

S-6. It's important that members of my family and close friends share my religious beliefs and values.

S-7. I believe that a person can be moral regardless of his or her sexual codes, etc.

S-8. I believe we were all put on earth to help each other.

S-9. I believe in an afterlife.

S-10. I consider myself a secular humanist.

INTELLECTUAL/CULTURAL

I-1. I love to go to the opera, ballet, and theater.

I-2. It's important that I have time to read every day.

I-3. I enjoy having music playing in the background when I'm working or relaxing.

I-4. I regularly take classes to improve my skills or learn something new.

I-5. It's important that I have opportunities to travel abroad.

I-6. For relaxation I enjoy movies and television.

I-7.   I am bored by museums and the theater. I'm a doer, not a watcher.

I-8.   I am uncomfortable in foreign environments.

I-9.   I enjoy cultural events that involve activities with others, such as ethnic festivals and dances.

I-10.   I enjoy salons or book groups where people share ideas.

ACTIVITIES/INTERESTS

A-1.   I love to garden.

A-2.   I want to act in a play.

A-3.   I enjoy tinkering around the house.

A-4.   I need to have pets.

A-5.   I like to take walks by myself.

A-6.   It's important to me that I always look my best.

A-7.   I prefer activities that take place outdoors.

A-8.   I'm very interested in artistic areas.

A-9.   I enjoy writing in my journal.

A-10.   I love to shop.

FRIENDS/COMMUNITY

C-1.   It is important to me that I live near my friends.

C-2.   I want to be involved in politics.

C-3.   I am committed to being involved in helping the less fortunate in my community.

C-4.   My friends are spread out all over the world, and I want the opportunity to visit them.

C-5.   I enjoy being involved with others in a community of interests (professional, political, cultural).

C-6.   It's important to me that I know and am close to my neighbors.

C-7.   I want to live in a group community setting.

C-8.   Community isn't very important to me. I prefer being with my family.

C-9. I enjoy having many friends and meeting new people.

C 10. I value my privacy and need time alone.

HEALTH/PHYSICAL FITNESS

P-1. Being fit is extremely important to me.

P-2. I exercise every day.

P-3. I am careful to eat a special diet for health.

P-4. I enjoy being active, but I don't have a set exercise program.

P-5. I don't think much about what I eat.

P-6. I have health problems that limit my mobility.

P-7. I need to have access to doctors and specialists.

P-8. My body and my look are extremely important to me.

P-9. Going to the gym and taking exercise classes are important parts of my life.

P-10. I eat only organic foods.

FINANCIAL/MONEY

M-1. Financial security is very important to me.

M-2. I want to make enough money so I can do what I want— travel, buy nice clothes, have a country home, etc.

M-3. I don't care about money as long as I have what I need.

M-4. I enjoy taking risks and playing the stock market.

M-5. It is very important that I save money for retirement.

M-6. Saving money isn't that important to me.

M-7. I would be willing to earn less money if I was doing what I truly enjoyed.

M-8. I am solely responsible for my support and the support of others.

M-9. I have a partner or family members who share expenses.

M-10. I prefer to have no credit card debt or loans.

CHAPTER 6

Making a Match

Achieving a Congruent Lifestyle

Now comes the important next step: matching your real life to your constellation of newly identified priorities. First, let me caution you: The constellation is an ideal. If there's someone out there whose actual life and "constellation of meaning" match exactly, I've never met him or her!

Having said that, don't be afraid to try. Most of us should be able to achieve some congruence—a balanced relationship between the things that are most important to us and the life we are actually leading.

What Drives You?

Review your solar system entries that are in the sun—your "heart's core" values—and also the entries you placed between Mercury and the sun. These are the values that you've chosen to shape your life—your organizing principles, if you will.

To get a rough-and-ready guide as to how your real life and your "constellation of meaning" mesh, assign each item inside the sun a value of 20 points, and each Mercury orbit item a value of 15 points. For this purpose, use both your Phase 1 and Phase 2 charts.

> **TIP:** Take your time. You may want to work on this exercise over a period of days or weeks.

Now take each item one by one and assign it an *actual* value. For example, one of the sun entries in the sample table is to have a child. If you have one, then both the ideal value and the actual value is 20 points. Whereas if you have no child, the ideal is 20 and the actual is 0.

Most items in your constellation won't be so clear-cut, and the numbers you assign will be approximations. Another item in the sample table is having a job that allows plenty of time for family. This is a core ideal—a 20. But work might force you to spend less time with your family than you would like, so you would place the number 10 in the Actual column.

There is plenty of variation in the scores individuals will attach to the same items. Let's say, for the sake of example, that your core desire is to own a sleek racing sailboat. It's right in the center of your sun—a 20. And let's say that you already have a perfectly serviceable, albeit unsleek, sailboat. You might

SAMPLE SUN/MERCURY TABLE OF VALUES

ITEM	IDEAL	ACTUAL
I want to have a child.	20	20
I want a job that allows plenty of time with my family.	20	10
I'd like to live in a house with a yard.	15	0
I want to be active in my church.	15	11
Financial security is very important to me.	15	7
Totals	85	48

find that the sailboat you have at least partially compensates for what you don't have, so you give yourself an actual score of 7. But maybe for you the sleek racing sailboat represents a desire so powerful that the serviceable sailboat doesn't even begin to compensate for not having it, so you put down an actual score of 2, 1, or even zero. (If you grew up hearing your parents say, "You should be happy with what you have," you may feel guilty for not being satisfied with your serviceable sailboat. But that's for another discussion—one you won't find in this book. Here we're talking about reality, not "shoulds.")

When you know what's real, what you truly value and want, you're much better able to make the decisions you need to make to construct a satisfying life—sometimes trading off one value or desire in favor of another.

In your notebook, make a chart like the one below, listing the items in or close to the sun, with their ideal values of 20 or 15; then estimate your actual values.

When you are done, total the two columns as in the sample list on page 113. Then, using a calculator, figure out in per-

SAMPLE SUN/MERCURY TABLE OF VALUES

ITEM	IDEAL	ACTUAL
Totals		

centage terms how much you actually have of what matters to you. Divide the "actual" score by the "ideal" score and round the number off to the highest percentage. This percentage represents how much of your ideal you have actually achieved. For the example given on page 113, here's the arithmetic:

48 (actual) divided by 85 (ideal) = 56%.

Now, evaluate the result using the following congruence scale:

75%–plus   Wow! You are one fortunate person, with an actual life that's very close to the way you want it to be.

65%–74%   For most people this score would constitute a very satisfying and fulfilling life. You have things to strive for but in the meantime you're basically content. Perhaps you can achieve one or more of your as-yet-unsatisfied desires; perhaps there are conflicts to be resolved and trade-offs to be made. But you're in a situation that allows you some choices in the matter.

50%–64%   Okay. Not a disaster, certainly, but you're not where you want to be, either. In the next chapter we'll look at how you can begin to make changes that will lead to greater satisfaction.

Below 50%   I'd say you're due for a major change. You don't have even half the things that really matter to you. But you've already made one extremely important step. You've established a picture of your goals and ideals. You've set out your priorities and now you can start to act. Read the following chapter for some practical ideas on how to begin.

People sometimes have funny reactions to this evaluation of the congruence between their ideal goals and their real life. A surprising number of people who have done this exercise find that they are more content than they knew. This knowledge seemed to free them up to actively make some changes. Even those who found a great deal of dissatisfaction and incongruence in their lives often felt exhilarated by having identified the problem and potential solutions. Nothing is more paralyzing than that vague discontent you can't name, or a longing that feels too distant to reach. The Solar System Technique can open a pathway for growth and change by making both your reality and your ideals tangible.

If, through charting your own solar system, you have recognized a serious lack of congruence between what you have and what matters to you, you need more than just breathing room to get out from under.

"Time for a Change," Part III, is for you. But first, let's talk about how to get started on change.

CHAPTER 7

Getting Started on Change
Take It One Step at a Time

The Solar System Technique has cleared a path to your true values and priorities—the things that really matter in your life. You've gotten a chance to look closely at how your day-to-day reality matches the things that are most vital to you, that are closest to your heart. It's a little nerve-wracking, isn't it? When you look at your charts and lists all laid out before you, and see where you stand on the congruence scale, you may now realize that you need to institute some changes to make room for what you have determined is most important to you.

The problem is, whether major or minor, the most difficult part of any change is knowing where to begin. The prospect of making changes to improve an overwhelmed, out-of-sync life can itself be a daunting challenge. Take heart. Here are some suggestions for how to begin.

To make significant improvements in your life, you are essentially going to war with some of your most ingrained habits, and if you're going to war, you'll need equipment and supplies. First, you'll need the lists you prepared of the entries in the sun/Orbit #1 grouping and the other orbit groups. You'll need your "congruence" charts, and you'll also want to have your Solar System Charts handy so that you can refer to them when working with your priorities, from your white-hot sun to the distant and cold planets circling the outer orbits of your interests. Second, I suggest you dedicate a loose-leaf notebook—with dividers—to keep track of all the organizing work you're doing using the Solar System Technique. And, finally, it's a good idea to use different-colored pens or markers to highlight and differentiate your work as you go through different stages.

BOAT—Activating the Tasks That Bring About Change

Everyone approaches problem solving and change differently, depending largely, I suppose, on personality. Some people prefer to begin with modest changes, and once those have been achieved, start focusing on the more central issues, those matters of greater import and concern. A helpful hint: Sometimes you get so tangled up in the little stuff that you never get to the really important things you set out to accomplish when you began the process. If you find this happening to you, set an "initiate" date for getting started on a crucial change to your overall organizational plan. Or you might prefer starting with an issue of major importance—such as looking for a new job— and begin your changes there.

Whatever your preference, I've devised a method to help you get started and keep going on your changes. The BOAT system is really a simple organizational tool for breaking very big life goals into a system of organized tasks. BOAT is an acronym for:

> Brainstorm.
> Organize.
> Add to daily task list.
> Time-spread.

Here's how it works. Begin by taking an item from Orbit #1 on your Solar System Chart—for example, "I want to work at home." Let's say that you've established a goal to start a desktop publishing business from home. But first, you need a state-of-the-art computer that will do the job.

Brainstorm.

Brainstorm every actual task that you can think of concerning buying a high-end computer. Be as specific as possible. For example:

- list features that are important to you (i.e., fast processor, high-capacity memory, audio/video features, graphics, word processing, modem, etc.)
- read magazines and shopping guides
- price models that fit your needs
- browse in computer stores
- test models
- browse ads
- update your skills
- solicit advice from friends and colleagues

And so on.

Organize.

Organize your tasks once you've figured out what they are. You can organize tasks by sequence or priority.

Most of the time your tasks should be placed in sequence: First I do this, then I do that, then I do that. For example, if you're buying a computer, your sequential list might be:

1. Decide which tasks you need your computer to perform—such as spreadsheets, word processing, graphics.
2. Investigate which computers have what you need.
3. Price the computers.

Add tasks to your Daily List.

This is the crucial link that will turn your wishes, hopes, and dreams into reality. Your Daily List is your guide to your day's tasks and your schedule. It's one of your prime time management tools, in fact. (See Daily List, page 22.)

So your goal of buying a computer will break down into tasks that you will gradually add to your Daily List, such as:

- Order a manufacturer's catalog.
- Buy a PC shopping guide.
- Call Joe and ask his advice.

Key: Systematically, over time, feed these goal-directed tasks into your Daily List until the goal becomes a reality.

Time-spread.

Even a change as seemingly straightforward as buying a computer can be stressful. In fact, for some people, choosing the right system may initially seem like a daunting task. So, time-

---

WHEN TASKS WON'T COME TO MIND

Sometimes our ideas seem to disappear when we're in the midst of brainstorming. Try these three brain jumpstarters to get your thinking juices freely flowing:

1. What are the ten things I need to do? Sometimes choosing a number will break the mental logjam.

2. Distance yourself. Tell yourself you're not going to do it, but if you were to do it, this is what you'd do.

3. Share the load. Brainstorm with one or two other people who understand what it is you're trying to do.

spreading is a crucial piece of the BOAT method. Spread the task out. Take your time. Decide to tackle one item each day—or even each week. Keep in mind that every significant change brings a shift in the balance of your life—expectations, costs, trade-offs, and gains. I often tell people that time-spreading is the most important piece of the BOAT method. That's because oftentimes the reason people give up on a goal, or feel paralyzed and uncertain, is because they try to do too much too soon.

Obviously, every change isn't as straightforward as buying a computer. But you can use the same premise for buying a house, relocating, or even planning to have a baby. (For example, if you're planning to have a baby, you might start with evaluating your financial resources, clearing out the spare room, interviewing nurses, etc.) The key is to break every seemingly overwhelming ideal into tasks you can actually accomplish that will move you in the direction of achieving it. This technique will serve you well no matter what you're trying to accomplish.

In order to fully take advantage of the Solar System Technique, you need to break the logjam and become an "option thinker." That is, the first questions you should ask whenever you are confronted by a seemingly overwhelming situation are "What are my options? Am I making automatic assumptions about my limitations rather than exploring my possibilities with an open mind?" Chances are, by the time you've finished doing your charts and evaluating the level of congruence in your life, you've already begun to see that you don't have to be trapped in a way of life that brings you little joy. In Part III, I'll show you how to open yourself to the possibilities that exist in some major areas of your life: the work you do, the way you relate, and the lifestyle you choose.

PART III

Time for a Change

CHAPTER 8

Doing What Matters
How to Do What You Love and Love What You Do

For most of us, the idea of doing what matters refers to our vocation—the engine that drives our lives. Your vocation is the compelling center of how you spend your days. It is usually some kind of work—although it may not be work in the conventional sense. For practical purposes, however, most of the difficulty people have in getting out from under concerns an incongruence in their work life, or a conflict between work life and other areas.

That's why the Solar System Technique is so effective. It takes into account the fact that work, family, home, finances, ideals, and other core factors all interrelate. It isn't possible to have the life you really want if you focus only on one arena.

Conventional career counseling focuses rather narrowly on the actual work one does and assumes the other pieces of life's puzzle will fall neatly into place. For that matter, most people choose career paths in high school or college that provide few clues to what their lives will actually look like. For instance, if you decide, "I want to be a doctor," what does that tell you about the organization of your life? Very little, actually. When you are finally immersed in the day-to-dayness of it, your choice may actually look quite different than you thought it would.

My clients often complain that even when they are doing

work they love, they feel dissatisfied, pressured, and frustrated. Usually, the reason is their failure to bring the work they love into some kind of congruence with other parts of their lives. When I take them through the Solar System Technique, they begin to visualize their personal universes as whole, rather than fragmented. This can lead to surprising revelations.

A client of mine, Jeremy, is a case in point. For several years, Jeremy had been building a relatively successful graphic design and advertising company. He was quite gifted, and had many clients—including several national companies. However, although he worked very long hours, Jeremy's business was often stalled because he absolutely had no desire or ability when it came to hustling new business. Eventually, he grew to hate his work and was quite concerned that he had chosen the wrong field.

Well, not exactly. After Jeremy did the Solar System Technique, he had a significant breakthrough. He loved the actual work he was doing—designing brochures and ads—but he hated all the other tasks that came with being independent, including generating new business. Jeremy realized that he was better suited to a company environment, where he could concentrate on the work he really loved and ignore the rest. He found a job at a small ad agency and experienced a tremendous sense of relief and *rightness* about his choice.

What has your Solar System Chart revealed to you about what gives you the most satisfaction at work? For instance:

1. Do you prefer to work alone or with others?
2. Do you prefer structured or unstructured work situations?
3. Do you prefer autonomy, or do you prefer strong direction?
4. Do you prefer a risky job, such as police work or firefighting, or one with few risks?
5. Do you prefer analytical, intellectual work? Creative work? Directing and managing others?

6. Do you prefer physical jobs? Or do you prefer more sedentary tasks?
7. Do you prefer to work indoors or outdoors?
8. Do you prefer helping professions, like social work or medicine?
9. Do you prefer jobs that allow you a lot of social contact or little?
10. Is it important to you to "make a difference"?

This is, above all, a book about making choices and exploring options. As you review your Solar System Chart, what do you learn about where you'd like to be? Think about that as we talk about some of the options.

Exploring Downshifting

Getting out from under usually means making some adjustments in your work life. Do you want more time to enjoy your life outside of work—your family, hobbies, and friends? Does it seem as though you're trapped on a perpetual merry-go-round and can't get off? It's the lament most commonly heard from overworked men and women everywhere.

Maybe you share Robert Reich's priorities. Just days after he announced his decision to resign as Secretary of Labor in the Clinton cabinet, Robert B. Reich, in an article published in the Op-Ed sections of the *New York Times* and *Washington Post*, wrote, "I have the best job I've ever had and probably ever will. No topping it. I also have the best family I'll ever have, and I can't get enough of them. Finding a better balance? I've been kidding myself into thinking there is one. The metaphor doesn't fit. I had to choose. I told the boss I'll be leaving, and explained why." Many people were stunned, since Reich's boss was the president of the United States. Still, his words resonated.

A week later, Deval L. Patrick, assistant attorney general

and the Clinton administration's chief civil rights enforcer, also announced his decision to quit. "My family's in Boston and I've been commuting to Washington for about two years," Patrick said. "This was a hard decision because I love this job. But I miss my kids and I love my wife, and I need to be home."

Are these examples merely blips on the radar screen? Or do they represent the beginnings of a serious trend toward what has come to be called "downshifting"?

Downshifting doesn't require that you head out to the North Woods to get away from it all. You may like your house and your car. You may enjoy dining out. You may want to continue taking vacations in the Caribbean. But spending time with your family and friends is vital to your mental health. And if that's the case, then downshifting may be for you—even if you have an exciting, demanding job that you love.

Downshifting is really about deciding that work is taking up too much of your time, and deciding to reduce the load and open up space for other areas of life that really matter. The change you make may be as small as a little tweaking of your schedule, or as major as changing your job. Here are three levels of increasing intensity, including some organizational techniques that can help make each a reality.

Level 1: Lightening Up

This probably applies to many people. You're reasonably satisfied with your life and work situation. What's needed is *less* of what you don't like and *more* of what you do. Michael, one of my clients, was in exactly this situation.

Michael worked long and hard to attain a senior position in a major accounting firm. He relished his work, but he wanted to cut back on his long office hours and frequent traveling so he could spend more time with his family.

This nagging desire remained vague and unformed in his

ARE YOU READY TO DOWNSHIFT?

1. In the last two months, have you been able to have dinner with your family only once or twice a week?

2. In the last two months, have you missed a family event such as a birthday, your child's school play, or a recital, because of work-related pressures?

3. Is there an activity you would love to do but can't because of work pressures?

4. Within the last two months, have you been away from home eight nights or more for business travel?

5. Do you find you don't have time to spend on social, civic, church, community, charitable, or cultural activities?

6. Is your work schedule creating pressures in your family?

7. Do you find yourself unable to spend time on hobbies or activities?

8. If there were a personal or family crisis, such as an illness or a death, would taking time off create tremendous stress or jeopardize your job?

If you answered yes to at least three questions, you may be ready to downshift.

mind—until an important business meeting made him miss his young son Jake's seventh birthday party. Michael called Jake to tell him he wasn't going to make it for his party. Both father and son were deeply disappointed.

That was the defining event for Michael. As much as he relished his job, he knew that life is short. Michael made the decision to find ways to spend more time with his family.

Plenty of busy, hardworking people have been in this situation. They, too, have figured out ways to tilt the demands of the job back in favor of their families. Like other harried parents before him, Michael set some goals for himself. From now on, he intended to:

- Be home in time for dinner at least three times during the workweek.
- Spend every weekend with the family. (In his autobiography, Lee Iacocca wrote that, throughout his career, weekend time was family time until Sunday evening. That's when he sat down with his planning book to write down his goals for the coming week.)
- Be present for all significant family events such as birthdays and anniversaries.

Easier said than done, you may be thinking. But Michael was willing to follow a set of specific strategies. I advised him to put seven techniques into action to get his work done and free up more time for his family, and he agreed to try the following:

1. Get an earlier start. Michael began arriving at his office forty-five minutes earlier than he normally had, three times a week. He found he could get far more work done in the quiet atmosphere of the early morning. Many effective managers have learned to do this. When his children were very small, John Reed, the famous chairman of Citibank, used to go into the office *very* early so that he could be home by six o'clock every evening. He wanted to spend time with his children while they were still awake.

2. Reorient the commuting routine to make productive use of previously wasted time. Michael stopped driving to work. Not only was it less stressful and harrying, but commuting on the train gave him two hours every day to read reports and make notes for new consulting projects. He soon discovered a related trick for lunch hour. Whenever he could, Michael closed his door at lunch and, while eating, used the time for reading and private work to help keep himself ahead of the curve.

Michael also got into the habit of seeking out short intervals during the day—ten minutes here, fifteen minutes there—for specific, quick tasks. He could write two or three e-mail messages, edit a report, go over the next week's agenda, or call his wife to see how her day was going. He was surprised by how much he accomplished in those circumscribed periods of time.

3. Change his working style. A lot of Michael's late-night meetings were spur of the moment. He was well liked and respected, so his colleagues frequently asked him to get involved in their projects. How many evenings had he quietly let himself into his sleeping household at midnight, welcomed only by a dozing pet? He decided to rethink his strategy. Instead of staying at the office late, or going out for long business dinners, Michael encouraged his colleagues to present their projects to him early in the morning.

4. Master preplanning. Prior to any significant family event, Michael made sure to review his calendar and schedule lists for projects or future deadlines that could in any way hinder a timely departure on the day of that celebration. As a result, Michael began the planning on *all* of his projects earlier. He also became astute at scheduling work carefully around key birthday and anniversary dates. He was delighted to discover that he was becoming generally more efficient by this close attention to detail, both in his life and his project planning.

5. Reduce business travel. By employing the latest available technology, using the Internet, e-mail, and videoconferencing, Michael was able to eliminate close to half of his previous business travel. This required considerable initial cooperation from his firm, which Michael succeeded in getting simply by making it a case of economics. When the firm realized the enormous cost savings he was able to produce by using teleconferencing and e-mail to do the same work he'd once done by traveling, they were sold. Michael's example caught on in the firm at large; he received high praise for successfully changing his firm's "culture of travel" to a culture of staying put.

6. Get extra help. The world is full of people who can lift some of life's more irritating and time-consuming jobs off our hands. Because they agreed to spend what little free time they had together relaxing rather than working, Michael and his wife learned to make more frequent use of hired hands. It was a win-win situation for everyone involved.

Previously, weekends had been eaten up with endless chores. Although the first few years they'd owned their house, raking the leaves in the autumn, mowing the lawn and pruning the shrubbery during the spring and summer, washing the car, cleaning the garage, clearing the gutters, all of it had been novel and fun. But, as time with the family became more precious, Michael and his wife contacted the local high school to find a teenager interested in making extra money. On Saturdays, a high school senior saving for college expenses now comes over and performs routine maintenance chores for a few hours, while the family does what it wants to do, instead of what they used to have to do to maintain their property and keep up with housework.

As long as you can afford it, there's nothing wrong with "outsourcing," finding someone to handle some of life's less agreeable tasks—cleaning, laundry, whatever it is that you personally detest doing yourself.

Level 2: Change Your Job

With this level you increase the intensity of change.

Who would give up a good, steady job? Who'd give up a job they already had for some other job they weren't at all sure about? Amos Mosley did. He'd been working twelve-hour days, seven days a week, for five years, as the day manager of a small convenience store. He had absolutely no time to spend with his family at home. As a last resort, he brought his wife and children into the store to restock the shelves and run the register while he took inventory and reordered grocery items. It finally became clear that putting everyone to work was not a solution to his family time problem.

He started looking through the classified advertisements in the newspapers and found a new job, working from 11 P.M. until 5 A.M., five nights a week. Because of the night shift differential, Amos was paid for forty hours while working thirty hours. His time problem was solved. He was able to be at home when his children left for school in the morning, and be there when they returned in the afternoon. His entire life changed. He was able eventually to go back to school and get a college degree, which led to an even better job a couple of years later.

Success stories like Amos Mosley's are becoming possible because employers are increasingly recognizing the need to offer flexible work schedules. If you're in a work situation that allows no flexibility or reduction in hours, you have a few choices:

1. Either resolutely remain with your current job, or,
2. Seek different work with fewer demands on your time, or,
3. Find one of the many jobs in which employers are willing to be flexible, so you might be able to arrange a schedule that works for you.

Kathy Wilson of Des Moines, Iowa, took the last route. After a promotion, her new position with a Norwest Credit Card Services Unit involved both managerial and training duties. But after more than four years of eighty-hour weeks handling both parts of the job, Kathy wanted a break—and she got it. Norwest allowed her to relinquish her managerial duties, while still holding onto the training aspects of her job. Her base pay was also reduced, but because she'd been with Norwest for four years, the difference was less important than the pension and benefits package she continued to receive.

In comparison, Susan, an investment banker in Chicago, knew that the nature of her work didn't allow for a change. Her eighty-hour workweeks weren't going to change. Susan downshifted by looking for a new job. Using her knowledge of finance, she landed a job as a columnist for a major business publication. She'd been the editor of her class literary magazine during her undergraduate years in college, and was intrigued at the idea of joining her financial expertise with her former literary interest.

This shift was possible after Susan's Solar System Chart revealed two things: First, she wanted her work to include a creative element. Second, she was willing to make a financial sacrifice in order to have a life that made her personally happier.

Instead of eighty hours, Susan is now working forty to forty-five hours a week. "I'm not making as much as I used to," she told me, "and I miss the money. But at least now I have a life. The tradeoff is worth it to me."

Susan had her solar system in order—her priorities were clear, and so she was able to make a smooth transition from one point in her career to another. She was also prepared for and comfortable with the change in income.

Level 3: Radical Change

Now we're moving into the realm of serious change. What if you were just to quit your full-time job? It does happen occasionally, of course, but it's not really necessary. The Solar System Technique is a guideline for breaking down your priorities and aspirations into manageable parts. Plenty of people are able to hold onto their full-time jobs while pursuing part-time work, or becoming self-employed, so a smooth transition can be made from one to the other.

For those unable or unwilling to maintain full-time careers, an entire corporate culture has sprung up that has integrated the concept of the "temp"—the long-term part-timer, sometimes paid more per hour, but without any benefits or credit given for length of employment—into the regular workplace. In certain situations, that suits many people.

If you haven't yet caught up with the trend, temping has changed a lot in recent years. It is no longer strictly the domain of the receptionist or secretary. Many companies use highly skilled temps to perform duties that were once performed by full-time employees. The flexibility of doing meaningful work on a temporary basis suits many people just fine. For example, Greg, an executive with an international trading firm in Seattle, took early retirement at age fifty so he could return to school and get an advanced degree in Japanese culture and language. He had been studying Japanese independently for many years and wanted to exploit that valuable skill. While he was at the university, Greg sometimes earned extra money by temping for firms around the city that needed assistance in drawing up business plans for development in Asia. Greg enjoyed the challenge, and by the time he was ready to start his consulting business, a number of firms he had temped for were eager to sign up.

Still, no matter how appealing the concept may seem, leaving the "regular" world of work for the less secure world of part-time work, temping, or self-employment is a radical change. If you decide that such a change is for you, there are a couple of issues you'll have to quickly face up to. They are, simply:

1. *Lifestyle*—What kind of life do you want to live? For many people, having the freedom to pursue their passions is more important than having a steady income. I know a very talented artist who works part-time in a clothing store to support her passion.

2. *Money*—There is almost always a price to pay for replacing steady income with less regular income. What are you willing to live without? Many families downshift right in the middle of their lives. Sid, Penny, and their two children lived in a fairly large city. Sid was a Certified Public Accountant who wrote murder mysteries on the side. Penny was a second grade teacher at the local elementary school. Sid announced that he was going to quit working at his job in the accounting business to write full-time instead. Penny supported him in this. They and their kids moved out of their house a few months later, and went to live in the small town where Sid had grown up. Penny got a job in the school there, and they bought a little two-family home, renting out the bottom floor. It was quite a change in lifestyle, especially for their two children, but everyone adjusted. They went to a new school, made new friends, and after a couple of years, one of Sid's books was sold and published!

Increasingly, workers are expressing the willingness to make sacrifices in the interests of doing the work that really matters to them. Recently, more than six hundred out of a thousand people interviewed by Robert Half International, a financial and technical recruiting company, stated that they would be willing to take a cut in pay if they were able to reduce their work hours and spend more time with their families.

Opportunities for Flexibility

Several current studies show that people are expecting more—including time, apparently. They consider what once were luxuries to be necessities, and they're willing to work longer hours to acquire them. Yet, paradoxically, people also want more leisure time to enjoy those luxuries, and are eager to find ways to cut or compress the number of hours they spend on the job. In response, many companies are adopting "flex-time" plans as cures for their chronic staffing problems—as well as compressed workweeks, job sharing, part-time work, and telecommuting. There's a cornucopia of choices available for almost all kinds of "highly desirable" workers—such as those in the computer software industry, hospital staffs, and legal secretaries. The list of flexible jobs is almost endless. Many companies view alternative work plans—four ten-hour days, or three twelve-hour days, for instance—as a way of reducing the increasing level of conflict employees are experiencing with the demands of work and family.

There has also been more of a merging of work and play, with the play being taken in smaller doses, while work is able to be accomplished almost anywhere. Technology has seen to it that we can literally be plugged in—by pager, phone, cellular phone, fax, computer modem, e-mail, the Internet, and even by videoconferencing—at almost all times. Certain work can be done almost anywhere—and is!

Employers are increasingly taking advantage of this technology, and see the sense in allowing their employees to devise their own work hours and work environments. Allowing

---

FIND MORE MEANING IN YOUR CURRENT JOB

You don't necessarily have to quit and get a different job to find meaning. Here are some small ways you can align what you already do to be closer to the sun in your Solar System Chart.

• Look for ways to be more productive. Sometimes we find ourselves in a rut, working automatically instead of being in the moment. If you focus on what you're doing and concentrate on the task at hand, not only will you be more productive, but time will fly.

• Is there some other facet of your job that you've never experienced? Ask your employer for a different job within the company, or see if you can expand what you do as part of your current job. Keep work interesting, and you'll stay interested.

• Change your schedule. Sometimes all you need is a slightly different perspective to discover that you prefer to work from seven to three, instead of the traditional nine to five. The variations are endless. Can you work at home? It's becoming an increasingly popular option in the cyber age.

• Redefine success. Are you a success, but miserable nevertheless? Examine your Solar System Chart.

---

employees to do their work with the greatest efficiency is a very appealing concept from a number of different viewpoints, both personal and corporate.

Working at Home

It is estimated by the Federal Bureau of Labor Statistics that, in 1998, more than 30 percent of the entire labor force was either self-employed or working from home, staying in touch with their main office primarily by computer. As this is a relatively new phenomenon, it comes attached with a number of pros and cons. The most important question is whether it suits you. Don't assume that just because you would like to spend less time at the office and more time at home, you can combine the two. The decision to work at home, or to do some of your work at home, should be made in conjunction with the other values on your Solar System Chart.

Having evaluated that, be aware of what you're getting into. For instance, for some reason home offices aren't taken as seriously as regular work sites, which are considered inviolate. Friends, family, and colleagues sometimes behave as though you have all the time in the world, because, after all, you're at home. So there's a credibility factor at work here, and it goes beyond just the personal interruptions that are suffered. Clients, as well, can be skeptical of your abilities if they hear children screaming in the background, a dryer running, a washing machine on the rinse cycle, or any other "household" noises. For many, not having a separate place of business makes credibility somewhat suspect, though with the increasing preponderance of businesses run from home, that particular prejudice is beginning to fade.

It certainly helps if you have certain rules of conduct that are understood by the entire household. Set boundaries and limits, and make your office a space where you can reasonably do business without interruption. It's critical to your success that you're able to establish and maintain a professional image.

A number of paging and telephone systems are currently available that can transform junior high school students into more sophisticated communicators than many a current home office. It's important to invest in a surefire system, so that all calls are answered in a professional manner and all messages are received and responded to. A well-designed phone and computer system can create a "virtual" office staff—dedicated fax lines, computer modems, e-mail, Internet traffic, and Web sites can connect an at-home office to the entire world.

One of the most important ways to provide a solid professional image for your work is to use the very best equipment—computers, faxes, laser printers, quality paper, the whole nine yards—because without it you'll be pegged as an amateur in an instant. It's also considered important to use a consistent design logo as your personal "corporate" identifier. Letterheads, business cards, mailing labels—all should share the same logo and design concept. Anything that looks fly-by-night is usually pegged as a less than professional operation and is quickly accorded amateur status. Designing your own marketing materials rather than having them professionally produced is a common error that you should try to avoid making. Pay attention

---

DOES HOME WORK SUIT YOU?

Check It Out on Your Solar System Chart

- Am I self-motivated?
- Am I disciplined?
- Do I have good work habits?
- Can I organize my work?
- Can I meet deadlines?
- Can I work alone?
- Can I work without direction?
- Do I have a support system?
- Do I have a room or area just for work?

If you answered yes to most of these questions, you should do fine working at home. Too many no responses may indicate that you wouldn't succeed at "home work."

to detail—people notice. (If you're computer savvy and have the capacity for laser printing, you can design your own labels and business cards.)

If you have an address that shouts "residence," such as 71 Cherry Hill Lane, you can always opt for a box at your local post office. You can also subscribe to a business address, signing up with a company that forwards client mail.

Also, if you have to meet with clients, don't end up sitting around your kitchen table. If you don't have a formal office space that's presentable, a local restaurant, even the local library, is preferable to your kitchen or even your perfectly nice living room. Local hotels sometimes have small private conference rooms that you can rent on a short-term basis. Think business, and think a certain degree of formality. The proper attitude, brought to whichever table you ultimately choose to bring it to, will determine the outcome of any meeting.

Many people who have decided to work at home are not prepared for another problem—isolation. They find that they are unable to consistently motivate themselves, stay focused on their goals, and accomplish their work without a team of others around them to give shape to and activate their efforts. For others, it's the absence of validation that shakes their confidence and distracts them from their aims. They feel unable to take the steps necessary to put their plans into action. They become distracted, depressed, and disheartened. Staying dedicated to the growth of their own business is a difficult thing to do without support of any kind. After all, they have only themselves to rely on for success or failure, and that, combined with the isolation, can produce a deep emotional strain.

If you work at home and are struggling with isolation, the first thing you must do is review your Solar System Chart and make sure working at home suits you.

Structure your time. Make yourself get up at the same time

every day. Make yourself shower and dress before going to your office at home. Talk to people on the telephone. Go out and take a walk, buy a newspaper, say hello to neighbors. Then go back to work.

There are business networking groups near you—look for their meetings in the calendar section of the local newspaper—that have been formed specifically to help individuals in business for themselves. Such a group often focuses on one member at a time, and everyone offers advice and ideas about that particular business venture. It goes a long way toward reducing the terrible feeling of isolation so many working-at-home people increasingly feel. If you're still feeling isolated, getting a pet that needs to be walked is a great way to focus elsewhere and provide a sense of structure to each day.

The Random Priorities Roulette Game

Structuring your priorities is the key to making working at home work for you. This is a game I originally picked up from Peg Bracken's book, *I Hate to Housekeep*. The rules for Bracken's Russian Roulette are simple. List all the unpleasant jobs you can think of that you've been putting off doing, and make sure to write each one on an individual slip of paper. Place the slips into a large container, and stir vigorously. Draw a slip at random. Do whatever job is listed, even if it's one of your all-time most-hated tasks—for example, "go through and clear out three file folders." Remember that you're playing a game, and that's what you drew. Gambler's honor should see you through. In a few weeks, you'll see that there's not much left to do. Not only your office but your brain will enjoy the lack of clutter.

My client Kathleen devised the random priorities game as a further adaptation of the original roulette game, and what I like most about it are the colored cards—pink, yellow, and blue. Silly, I know, but tossed in a large glass jar, it's colorful.

KATHLEEN'S RANDOM PRIORITIES RUSSIAN
ROULETTE GAME RULES

- Write short tasks requiring fifteen minutes or less on
  the blue cards.
- Write tasks taking thirty minutes to an hour on the
  pink cards.
- Write more complicated tasks requiring the good part
  of a morning or an afternoon on the yellow cards.

The rules of the game can be adapted at this point to suit
your specific needs. Every day of her workweek, Kathleen
would shake the card jar, and pull a handful of cards out, separate one blue card, and place the rest back in the jar. Reading
the card, she'd then set about performing the task written on it,
trying to finish within her self-imposed fifteen minute deadline.
Later that day, usually after lunch, she'd repeat the process,
separating out one more blue card and following its direction.

Three days of the week, when Kathleen felt she'd have
more time, she'd draw a pink card, and try to complete the task
indicated on it within a half hour's time.

And one day each week, Kathleen blocked out an entire
morning or afternoon, drew a yellow card, and tried to perform whatever task she'd randomly assigned herself.

Kathleen never stopped making adjustments. To keep the
game interesting, she sometimes broke up some of the yellow
card tasks into smaller bits, which she would spread among the
blue and pink cards according to how long she thought a particular job might take. When she was wrong, she'd write the
task on a different-colored card and drop it back into the jar. I
highly recommend this game—it's fun, it's effective, and it
clears clutter.

Practical Matters

So, you've decided to get out from under. Can you reduce the number of hours you spend working each week without reducing your take-home pay? Is there any way to ensure against financial disaster when you decide to change your priorities? Of course there is, but it certainly isn't easy. It requires substantial foresight and planning to accomplish the transition successfully. What's of vital importance to you? Without a carefully constructed plan, you'll have no idea how much you should be saving for your coming transition, or how long you can carry it out before running out of funds.

Second, before you can downshift, you have to consider downsizing. Start taking a hard look at ways you can economize. Can you lower your car insurance payments? Live in a less expensive home or apartment? Dine out less often, and buy less expensive brands of groceries? There are dozens of ways to set aside money when you're following a plan.

Hopefully, doing the Solar System Technique and articulating your goals provoked an evaluation of your finances. If your priorities have changed in an important area of your life—work, lifestyle, or family—chances are you'll need to make financial concessions. Break down your finances, so you have a clear picture of how much money is coming in and how much money is going out each month. That, at a minimum, is an essential piece of knowledge when you're figuring out how to adjust for the difference in income that a change in priorities will often cause.

CHAPTER 9

Living in Sync

Repaving the Family Track

You've performed the Solar System Technique, and you now have a better idea of what really matters to you. However, if you are like many people, especially women, you may have uncovered a seemingly insurmountable conflict at your heart's core. That is, having children and reaching the top in your career are both centered squarely in your sun. This is not the kind of conflict that is easily resolved—sun conflicts never are.

Increasing numbers of working mothers, and some fathers, who are anxious to spend more time with their children opt for part-time work, a choice that more professionals in many fields—and more and more businesses—are making every day. There's a great level of flexibility on both sides of the equation with part-time work. For the businesses, there is the advantage of not having to provide benefits or pensions; they are thus able to pay higher hourly wages to part-time employees. For the workers, there is greater convenience and control. They may give up benefits on one end, but gain freedom on the other. It's a difficult choice for many people to make, especially when your employer is providing an excellent benefits package that includes health insurance, education credits, and a pension plan.

Dorothy had been a practicing lawyer for eight years, and she was a junior partner with a medium-sized law firm that specialized in litigation law. She got married, had a beautiful baby girl, Lillian, but kept right on working full-time. She knew she had to make a change the day she came home to find her nanny beaming with pride. The nanny ushered Dorothy into the TV room and turned on the VCR. Her wonderful nanny had grabbed a video recorder and filmed the baby's first steps earlier that day for Dorothy and her husband to view that night. Dorothy burst into tears when she saw her baby take her first steps—on TV! That really tore her up. Her husband wasn't too happy that he'd missed that moment, either, but it really got to Dorothy in a big way. She longed to spend more time with her child. At the same time, Dorothy knew that her work was part of her sun. If she quit her job and stayed home full-time, she was sure she'd be miserable, and that wouldn't be good for either her or Lillian.

Dorothy decided that she would try and balance her two important life priorities. She began to set in motion a plan to adjust her work schedule.

1. She negotiated an understanding with her firm that, for now, she would take on a "back office" role that would require many fewer meetings and would give her greater control over her schedule. A financial sacrifice was involved, but a manageable one. Yes, Dorothy was on the "mommy track." She readjusted her schedule.

2. Dorothy started coming into the office at least one hour earlier than in the past, and leaving by late afternoon. In this way, she'd be able to spend more time with Lillian, and yet accomplish her work.

3. She would spend more time with her daughter, but also make sure to schedule time for activities that had always

interested her—keeping up on legal journals and getting more involved in the community.

4. She would start to shop for and cook dinner at least three evenings each week. Dorothy also had some ideas about home renovation and decorating that she'd been thinking about for a long time. She decided to use some of her time to act on her ideas.

5. Because she wasn't giving up her work entirely, she vowed to carefully avoid the fate of friends who had traded in their careers only to find themselves essentially working as full-time, unsalaried chauffeurs—driving kids to preschool and after-school activities, car pooling, picking up groups from ballet and peewee hockey and transporting them hither and yon. It wasn't easy, because she wanted Lillian included in the whirl of little children's activities, and that required some sacrifices. Dorothy found herself volunteering to drive a group of the neighborhood children on Saturday mornings, the only morning of the week she really had free. She set up a schedule with the other mothers so that during the week her daughter got picked up and dropped off from her play dates and other activities, in exchange for Dorothy's weekend driving.

I recall Dorothy telling me about a friend who'd called her trying to arrange a transportation schedule a few weeks before. "Now, Ashley has to be at Madame Nijinsky's Ballet Academy for her 8:40 A.M. barre class," the woman told Dorothy, reading from a list. "Nicole has to be at Warren Le Tang's Tap Dance Emporium at 9 A.M.—on the nose—for her Fosse jazz tap tutorial, and Bogart—that's the little redhead in the corner, with the thick glasses and the wet pants—has to be at Captain Eddie's Music Studio at 9:15 for his slide guitar lesson. Can you handle it? Or should we try to get Ashley's mother out of surgery again to drive her little baby to ballet?" Dorothy joked that it was probably only her years of experience in litigation that enabled her to successfully negotiate her chauffering duties. And she *was* able to get all of the children to their lessons on time, including her own!

Dorothy's husband wholeheartedly supported her decision to cut back on her workload. By deciding to gear down and temporarily limit her workload, many of the things they'd wanted to do while still a young family became possible.

To her delight, Dorothy quickly discovered that there were entirely unforeseen benefits to her decision. She became much more efficient at work, quickly able to delegate the research and the noncentral issues of her caseload to her subordinates. She had an excellent paralegal and an exceptional legal secretary; she soon found that, while she was spending more time at home with her family than ever before, her legal career was running more smoothly than ever before. Her priorities had forced her to institute changes she may not have otherwise made. She managed to continue to do something she loved while being able to have more time to give love to the people who were most important to her.

Planning the Family Track

Okay, let's get practical. You and your spouse are happily pursuing meaningful careers, but you want to have a family too. Advance planning is key. Too many families are completely caught off guard by the demands of child raising.

Hint: Even if your company is family friendly, and your boss assures you that you'll have his or her full support, do your own planning. Your boss's primary focus is the job at hand—not making your life more convenient. He or she will appreciate your efforts to make things run more smoothly.

CAN YOU AFFORD THE FAMILY TRACK?

1. Evaluate the work that you do. Does it involve a traditional "ladder," where you rise from rung to rung over a period of years? Or is it more flexible?

2. If your answer is the first, you need to face some hard choices. It may not be possible to combine work and family and still achieve your goal. Brainstorm other possibilities within your field that would involve satisfying work but be less linear. Or make the decision to delay children until you have achieved the level that is your goal.

3. If your career path involves flexibility, make a list of options. Does your career allow you to work at home or part-time?

4. Can you take a hiatus without jeopardy?

5. Does your spouse have flexibility in his career that will make it easier to share parenting duties?

6. Are you employed in a field, such as nursing, that allows flexibility in hours?

7. Will it enhance your career to go back to school? A part-time school schedule might be more easily combined with parenting.

1. Review Your Solar Systems

Don't expect that you and your partner will necessarily have the same expectations about parenting. After all, you grew up in different households, with different sets of parents, whose styles may have varied widely. I've found that many couples simply assume that because they are committed to their relationship, they'll automatically agree on every important issue. Not true. Reviewing and discussing your individual solar systems will help you be more realistic. Look for these clues:

FAMILY PLANNING TIPS

DON'T assume that a child won't change your lives. Plan ahead so you won't be caught off guard when you hit the first barrier.

DO work out the details. Who is responsible for what? Chaos loves a vacuum.

- Is having a child close to your sun, but farther out on your partner's system—or vice versa?
- Do you and your partner agree that it is very important for you to share equally and fully in parenting?
- What are your individual financial priorities? Children are expensive, and there may be other trade-offs as well if you decide that one of you should stop working or work part-time.
- Do you believe that good day care is a healthy and positive thing, while your partner strongly believes that a child should be with a parent full-time in the early years?
- How flexible are each of you regarding unconventional arrangements? Do your employers support both mommy *and* daddy tracks? Is one of you willing to put your career on hold for a few years to be a primary caretaker for your children?

2. Brainstorm Your Options

Once you've become clear on what each of you needs to make the family-career juggle work, the next step is to consider your options. I think the best way to go about brainstorming is to put every option you can think of on the table—without regard initially to its value. Some of the items on your list may seem outlandish, but that's okay for now.

Once you have your list of options, the next step is to rank them in order of feasibility. For example, Jack and Susan, a young career couple I enlisted for this exercise, created an option chart that looked like the chart shown here.

Workable Options	Possible Options	Unworkable Options
• Six months of family leave for Susan.	• Jack can take on more freelance work to give him time at home.	• Susan can stop working.
• Day care in a neighborhood home run by a friend of Susan's.		• Jack can stop working.
• Jack's mother cares for the baby three days a week, the other two in day care.	• Move to a less expensive neighborhood so Susan can afford to work part-time.	• Hire a live-in nanny.
• Wait three years for Jack to establish a home business.		

3. Have a Plan

Once you have children, you'll need to keep adjusting your scheme. Children have a way of foiling even the best-laid plans. You can reduce the chaos by having a strategy for every inevitability—a sick child, a school emergency, a teacher's strike, a snow day, etc., that might require a backup plan.

A Successful Family Track

When Paul and Ellen decided to start a family, they were not caught off guard by the realization that their lives would be turning upside down. As Ellen observed, "I think one of the reasons people get into so much trouble juggling jobs and kids is that they didn't think they'd have to make that many changes when they had kids. Believe me, life cannot go on as before."

I thought Ellen's insight was extremely important. The much-hyped "having it all" motif for women has had to be readjusted as families faced the practical realities of child raising. Ellen told me, "I didn't want to sacrifice my work, which I loved, but I also didn't want to be one of those crazed women, rushing from home to work, and doing neither job well."

Paul's attitude was that "This isn't just a woman's issue. I felt that my involvement was just as important. When I was growing up, my brothers and I spent most of our time with our mother because Dad was always at work. I wanted my kids to know me, and I wanted to know them."

Paul and Ellen shared a philosophy that helped them make decisions about their family. Both of them defined the "good life" as having balance. Neither saw themselves as driven workhorses who put their jobs above all else. But at the same time, both believed that they would be better parents if they were also allowed to pursue their personal goals.

Paul was part of a new wave of baby boomer men who were willing to take a new approach to work. "It used to be that a man had to sacrifice family time to be successful in his job," Paul said. "I think the opposite is true. Men make better managers when they bring their parenting skills into the workplace."

A study by John Snarey, a psychologist at Emory University in Atlanta, appears to support Paul's belief. In his book *How Fathers Care for the Next Generation* (Harvard University Press), Snarey reports on a study of 240 fathers conducted by Harvard University over a period of forty years. The study shows that by midlife, devoted dads on average were more likely to thrive in their careers, as well as have happier marriages.

Devoted fathers in the study went on to become involved in

care-giving activities outside the home, as managers, mentors, coaches, or community leaders. Snarey says that parenting provides skills and a perspective that just aren't available elsewhere. Fatherhood can build mentoring skills, which can be used in the workplace—for example, supervising younger employees.

Solving Work-Family Conflicts

Here is a practical method for beginning to get a handle on your work-family conflicts.

Make a List

Set aside some time to brainstorm. You can do this alone, or with your spouse or a friend. Make a list of the things that pull you in two directions. Put them in two columns, one for work and one for home. Then see if you can group similar factors into a few problem areas. The evening phone calls, take-home projects, and extra work hours all relate to overtime on the job, for instance.

Think About Your Options

After you've made your list, consider the big and little changes you could make to address each of the problem areas. Potential drastic changes might include quitting your job and seeking a more empathetic employer, switching to part-time work, or moving to a city where you have relatives willing to help with your kids. You might not be able or willing to take any of those steps, but thinking about big changes can help you identify the little things that also could make your life easier.

Network Your Neighborhood

Put together some emergency child-care plans where you live now. Is there a retiree in your neighborhood who would like to pick up some extra income by sitting for your sick child? Are there others who might be available on short notice—a stay-at-home mother with older children, for instance?

Talk to Your Boss

Be honest with your boss about how work is interfering with your family life after hours. Is every late-night phone call and last-minute project something that really can't wait until the next day? What's the worst that can happen if you turn on the answering machine and stop taking business calls at night?

Take One Step at a Time

Don't try to tackle every issue on your list at once. Eliminating even one or two stress inducers can make a big difference. But don't abandon the list after you solve one or two problems, either. Make time every few weeks to check the list and tackle another issue. And update the list when new problems arise or old ones are eliminated.

Finally, be sure to update your Solar System Chart from time to time. Your life will change as your children grow and priorities shift.

CHAPTER 10

Coming Home
Finding the Perfect Fit in Lifestyle and Community

Every day I receive feedback from my clients, from readers of my newsletter, and from groups I speak to, suggesting that a big reason people have trouble coping is that their basic lifestyle—that is, where and how they live—doesn't support their needs, preferences, and dreams. Furthermore, the fragmentation of communities adds extra stress; people complain that services aren't available or convenient, that they don't know (much less work with) their neighbors, and that commuting adds long hours to already lengthy days. The list goes on.

Yet many people tend to feel that where and how they live are the arenas that contain the least number of choices. I frequently hear comments like these:

"I would love to live in the city, but I could never afford it."

"We've always dreamed about moving to the West Coast, but our families are here."

"I wish I could get rid of this big house and buy a condo, but the market is lousy."

"Commuting adds three to four hours to my workday, but our kids are in a good school, so moving is out of the question."

"My apartment building is so noisy, I can't think straight. I feel like I'm living in a frat house, but it's all I can afford."

These long-suffering statements are reflective of the sense many people have that they are trapped in their environments. While it is true that sometimes trade-offs are necessary in order to attain more important goals, I find that more often people simply haven't examined their assumptions. For example, when I asked Jim, a commuting father, to probe a little deeper, he acknowledged that he hadn't considered any of the following:

• His commuting schedule made him essentially an absentee father, and his presence in his children's lives was just as important (if not more so) as providing financial security for them.
• While the school in their town was very good, there might also be good schools in other places closer to his job.
• There might be satisfying job opportunities for him closer to home.

And so on. The Solar System Technique helps to break the mental paralysis by objectifying all the possibilities and placing lifestyle choices back in context.

Finding Home

Where and how you live—your lifestyle—is the underpinning of everything else in your life. If you weren't consciously aware of this before, doing the Solar System Technique no doubt demonstrated quite clearly that if you hate the way you live or the place you live in, none of the other aspects of your life really works.

Like many bright, career-oriented young couples, Holly and Steve decided to move from the relatively benign plains of Wichita, Kansas, to the urban center of Washington, DC, in order to pursue better opportunities—Steve as a congressional aide, and Holly as a public relations company account executive. They rented an apartment in the trendy Dupont Circle area, and they enjoyed exploring the city and being part of a fast-paced culture. After five years, however, the bloom was definitely off the rose. Their apartment, which they once thought of as "charming," was now just cramped. Their noisy street—exciting at first—was a migraine-producing environment. Although the city offered many conveniences, it didn't offer some of the things they realized they needed most—space, privacy, quiet, and a connection with the earth. Holly, an inveterate gardener, grumbled that window boxes and houseplants just didn't cut it. Steve, a runner, was growing tired of breathing in the fumes of a million auto exhaust systems when he took his morning run. They both loved dogs, but their building had a strict policy against pets. And they were starting to talk about having a family, which they knew would require a dramatic change in lifestyle.

Steve and Holly faced a dilemma, however. At first, they had considered moving into one of the many suburban areas that feed off the nation's capital. But housing prices were outrageous, and they knew that if they went that route, they would essentially become slaves to a mortgage. They wanted more than that out of their lives, but they weren't really clear on what.

When they sat down to do the Solar System Technique, they realized that their priorities had undergone a shift during their years in Washington. When they first moved from Kansas, their major focus was on their careers. They were happy to make sacrifices in order to pursue career opportunities. But now that their careers were more settled, and they'd had experience that was transferable elsewhere, they saw that their focus was more heavily weighted toward lifestyle. Rather than living in a setting that supported certain jobs, they now wanted to find jobs that allowed them to live in a certain setting.

This, by the way, is an example of the dynamic design of the Solar System Technique, and why you need to do it at least every few years as your priorities shift.

"The breakthrough came when we started to take another look at Wichita," Steve said. "We never thought we'd go back there, but now it seemed ideal in so many ways. It was a small city, but quite progressive, with some challenging government opportunities. Our families lived there. And there were some beautiful communities where you could buy a house for about a third of what it would cost in the suburbs of Washington."

So Holly and Steve went home. They traded big-city opportunities for a more manageable and ultimately—for them— more fulfilling life.

A more dramatic example of a change in priorities is the lifestyle change made by Marilyn Abraham and her husband, Scott MacGregor. I knew Marilyn from the days when she was a prominent senior editor with Simon and Schuster. She was the very essence of a sharp, committed career woman; since she and Scott were both publishing executives, their life was lived on the run. But a few years ago, after accumulating fifty-two years in publishing between them, Marilyn and Scott began to feel restless. They wanted to experience something entirely new before they were too old to enjoy it. So they purchased an RV and set off on a year's journey across America, before finally settling down to a new and less harried life in Santa Fe, New Mexico. Marilyn even wrote a book about their experiences,

First We Quit Our Jobs: How One Work-Driven Couple Got on the Road to a New Life (Dell, 1997). Always in tune with the trends, Marilyn realized that their saga would resonate among many burned-out professionals.

If doing the Solar System Technique revealed a restlessness that you are curious about following—or, simply, a dissatisfaction with the way you are currently living—this chapter will provide the opportunity to examine it. It all boils down to where and how you live—which plot you carve out for yourself from the enormous universe of choices.

Finding Your Lifestyle Fit

Sal and Beverly lived in a small two-bedroom rental house in a suburb of Atlanta. They were both doing well in their careers, and they had reached a point where they were able to buy a house. For the first time, they began giving serious thought to the kind of home environment they wanted. Since they had never dwelt on the topic before, they found it difficult to pinpoint the ideal setting for what they hoped would be a permanent home.

The Solar System Technique helped them to unblock some of their life themes, and thus provided important clues.

For example, Sal and Beverly had long ago made the decision that they did not want to have children of their own. However, they both realized that it was important to them to be in an environment where they could interact with children. That discovery led to a second revelation: It was important to them to live in a community where they knew and interacted with their neighbors.

However, another major theme of their lives seemed to be in conflict with this idea. Both Sal and Beverly had demanding full-time jobs, and they knew from their current experience that it was almost impossible to make friends in the neighborhood. It seemed that the people who were around during the day became very friendly with each other, as did the families with children. But they were pretty much excluded.

Then Beverly remembered an article she had read about a new trend in housing developments, called co-housing. Co-housing developments are built with the participating home-owners acting as the primary developers. On a given plot of land, houses are built in such a way as to foster cooperation and interaction. The fronts of the houses are built to face a common courtyard area and run along a pedestrian walkway, encouraging a feeling of neighborhood among the families. The focal point of all co-housing communities is the Common House. Here, residents can share meals, hold meetings, run a day care center, and have a place for social and recreational activities. Co-housing developments allow complete freedom and privacy to families and individuals, while also fostering community.

Sal and Beverly began to look into co-housing and discovered that two developments were being planned for their area. They bought into one that was nearly completed, and recently moved in. The development included several families with children, including a gay couple with an adopted child, two senior citizens, several singles, and one other couple that was married

---

LEARN MORE ABOUT CO-HOUSING

The husband and wife architecture team of Kathryn McCamant and Charles Durrett spent a year studying the first co-housing project built in 1972 outside Copenhagen, Denmark, and published a book about it, *Cohousing: A Contemporary Approach to Housing Ourselves* (Ten Speed Press, 1988).

SENIOR LIVING: A NEW RANGE OF CHOICES

Senior citizens have been living in "retirement" communities, especially in Florida, Arizona, and California, for years, but there are now more options available to them than there have ever been before. Co-housing is often perfect for retirees who want to stay in the mainstream, who want children and young families around them, and who want a diverse community to belong to that also offers some services, such as shared meals and planned social and recreational activities.

Other senior citizens prefer living among their peers in assisted living communities, where they maintain their autonomy but have the option of having housekeepers and home care aides, as well as on-site nursing facilities and meals prepared and brought in to their apartments. A third, increasingly popular option is the senior group homes put together by social service agencies. In New York City's Staten Island borough, a large, renovated Tudor-style home has been converted by Richmond Senior Services, a nonprofit agency, into housing for a dozen older residents. The residents pay $1,000 a month for meals, a room, towels, and sheets. Heavy cleaning, like vacuuming rugs and cleaning windows, is taken care of, but there are no medical facilities on site.

---

and childless. From the start, they all shared a common bond in a place that allowed as much or as little interaction as they wanted.

Homesharing

Homesharing is, as its name implies, an arrangement in which two or more unrelated people share a house or an apartment. Everyone shares common areas, like the kitchen and living room, but each person has personal space, usually a bedroom, where privacy is guaranteed. Homesharing was once the primary domain of college students and young working people. But it has been reinvented as a reasonable alternative for midlife and older people.

Kate and her husband, Mel, had lived in a spacious house in the lovely suburban community of Rye, New York, for forty-five years. They purchased the house when they were a young married couple, and had raised their two children there. When Mel died of a heart attack at the age of seventy-two, Kate, now sixty-eight, decided she had to sell the house, but she hated the idea of living in an apartment by herself. Her eldest daughter, Maureen, who lived with her husband and three children in upstate New York, urged her to move in with them, but Kate was adamant about not doing that. She didn't want to be part of her daughter's bustling household. Although she loved being a grandmother, part-time was just fine for her. Kate also wanted to remain in Rye, or at least close by, where she had friends, a church, and an active involvement in local life.

One day, she saw a notice on the community bulletin board that a woman in town was looking for another woman to share a small house, which had once been the carriage house of a large mansion. Intrigued, Kate called the woman and went to visit the property. Celine was seventy, and she had been widowed for ten years. The house was tiny, but it had two separate bedrooms and a wide front porch overlooking Long Island Sound. Kate fell in love with the setting, and she liked Celine. Best of all, her share of the rent would be only $600.

It had never occurred to Kate to consider sharing a home with another adult who was not a member of her family. And although she was intrigued by the idea, she didn't want to jump in without knowing Celine better. She worked out an arrangement with Celine to spend a couple of weeks living there while she put her house on the market.

It was an adjustment, at first—especially getting used to the tight quarters. But both women were respectful of each other's privacy, and they had enough in common to enjoy each other's company. It turned out to be a lucky find for Kate. She has now lived in the house with Celine for three years, and she is the envy of the seniors group at her church.

Finding Community Where You Are

I've discovered that many people use a much looser definition of community than we're used to. For them, community is not a place, nor is it a settled group. Community can exist wherever sharing happens—whether it's a chat with like-minded people

---

ARE YOU A CANDIDATE FOR HOMESHARING?

Homesharing is certainly not for everyone. But if it's something you might want to consider—even temporarily—look for a homesharer whose situation complements yours. For example, an older home-owner with a mortgage to pay off might want to share with a young couple trying to save money to buy a home. A person with a hearing disability might want to share with someone who has good hearing.

Refer to your Solar System Chart to determine whether you are suited to living with another person or persons. Also think about your previous experiences living with friends or relatives. Were they positive? Did you enjoy interacting with people every day? Was it relatively easy for you to compromise and be flexible to the needs of others?

It's very important that, like Kate, you try out a situation before you commit to it. That's really the only way you'll know if the fit is right.

on the Internet, regularly tuning in to a favorite talk radio station, or maintaining a link with old friends in other cities.

Community isn't necessarily a permanent thing, either. If you have young children, you might be involved for a few years with a community of mothers who share common issues. Later, you might move on to a different community—a group raising funds for the local library, or a book club.

Getting Practical: How to Finance a Move

Matthew and Eileen were a mid-thirties professional couple with a three-year-old son. Matthew worked as a middle-level executive with the telephone company. Eileen was a pediatric nurse. They had been living in a small two-bedroom apartment in Brooklyn, New York, during the six years of their marriage, but their goal was to be able to afford a house with a yard in a suburb of the city—either Long Island or Westchester County. When Matthew and Eileen did the Solar System Technique, they saw how important that goal really was. A family home in which to raise their son, with room for a second child, had white-hot "sun" meaning to both of them. However, with only about $12,000 in their joint savings account, they felt very far from their goal.

When I first interviewed Matthew and Eileen, I discovered that they were afflicted by a paralysis that often hits people when they can't see a way clear to their goals. Instead of making step-by-step plans, they were feeling defeated. "Maybe we'll win the lottery," Eileen laughed, and she was only half joking. This couple believed that nothing short of a major windfall would get them into a house.

Using the BOAT method, I walked them through a practical strategy that brought their dream down to earth where they could work with it.

Brainstorm

First, Matthew and Eileen did some brainstorming about what their ideal living situation would be: location, size, and style of home, proximity to services, schools, and so on.

Next, they researched the market. This included taking trips on the weekends to nearby communities, driving around, visiting real estate agencies, and attending open houses. (This was also a form of brainstorming.)

Organize

Armed with a good sense of what they wanted, what was available, and the range of prices, they organized their strategy: Decide how much home they could afford; get preapproved for a mortgage by a bank; hire a broker; and so on.

Add Tasks to Daily List

Matthew and Eileen discovered that they could afford a house in the range of $150,000—90 percent of that financed by a mortgage. Suddenly the idea of buying a house—albeit a small one, or a fixer-upper—didn't look so daunting. And when they turned the items on their list into actual tasks (make an appointment with a broker, open a dedicated bank account, etc.), they were able to check at least one item off the list every day so that they could see themselves moving toward their goal.

Time-spread

Matthew and Eileen avoided getting overwhelmed by this big step in their lives by spreading the tasks over several months—adding and checking off items as they went. Eight months after they began their search, they were moving into their first house.

When you use the Solar System Technique, the impossible becomes achievable, and the climb less steep.

Keeping Your Solar System in Motion

Let the great world spin forever down the ringing grooves of change . . .
—*Alfred, Lord Tennyson*

The greatest lesson we can take away from our use of the Solar System Technique is the sure reaffirmation that life is about change. We all know what goes on. People begin quietly drowning in the minutiae of their lives. They become overwhelmed by the detritus they've created, stressed out by their uncertainty and indecision as to what to do about it all. They end up frozen by their inability to clear all the "noise" out once in a while, to find an open, silent space where they can take a deep, centered breath.

Consider what happens when you organize a closet. For a few weeks—much longer, if you don't have kids!—everything stays just as you put it. It's all shipshape. But gradually, a hanger out of place here, a pair of shoes carelessly dropped over there, a couple of new purchases left in bags put in the back of the closet—you get the picture. And you know the inevitable result.

The same thing happens in most people's lives. The Solar System Technique is a way to stay on top of the clutter.

Your Solar System Chart can become the compass that helps guide your choices during the important moments of your life. For example, use the chart:

- before you get married, in order to make sure you and your partner are in sync on the important issues
- before you make a major purchase, such as a house or a car, in order to determine where the purchase fits into your overall financial plan
- before you start a family, in order to make sure you're in agreement on the parenting style and breakdown of responsibilities
- before you change jobs, in order to evaluate how the move fits into your long-term career plan

The Solar System Chart can also guide you when a major change occurs unexpectedly such as a divorce, a death in the family, a job layoff, or a sudden business opportunity.

Here are a few final suggestions for keeping what really matters front and center in the months and years to come:

MAKE JUST ONE CHANGE A YEAR

Don't bite off more change than you can chew. If you start with just one step toward your goal, it will be easier to take the next step after that.

- Lose twelve pounds.
- Get up twenty minutes earlier every day.
- Join a book club.
- Sign up for a class in a topic that will further your goals.
- Start work one hour earlier and leave the office at 4:00 instead of 5:00.
- Set up a filing system.
- Visit a part of the country you've always wanted to see.
- Paint one room in your house.
- Open a savings account for a trip, a house, a sabbatical—and contribute to it once a month.

Monthly Review

By keeping an organization and goal journal handy, you can make great headway on getting yourself out from under. Setting the goal of a monthly review is a pragmatic way of assuring yourself that your plan for certain changes is not only in motion, but being accomplished. It may be a bit at a time, but remind yourself that nothing of value is ever accomplished without a sustained effort. Keep your morale up. A journal allows you to see it in black and white.

Annual Evaluation

It can take you as little as half an hour to do an annual evaluation of your solar system, especially if you've faithfully kept a monthly record of your efforts. Choose a special day—your birthday, perhaps, or the last or first day of the year. I once read that Diane von Furstenberg sets aside a few hours every New Year's Day—which is also her birthday—to reflect on the previous year, and decide her priorities for the year ahead. She goes off by herself to a solitary place that allows the physical and mental space to really think. Her annual evaluation became an essential ritual.

The annual evaluation allows you to reexamine your choices, and to make any changes that you deem necessary at that time. Fine-tuning of time management and unconscious organizing habits kick into gear if you've been employing them long enough to have seen them make a significant difference in your lifestyle, habits, and work patterns.

Long-Term Plan

Long-term plans can include everything from a college fund for little Timmy to a dedicated savings plan for a down payment on a house. It may not be possible for you to make a big change right now. But that doesn't mean there are not countless small steps you can take on the road to that change. For example, you may set up a five-year plan to make a career change that includes training, financial management, and a physical move. Planned over a period of several years, your goal—which might have once seemed unattainable—is reachable through a series of practical steps.

The key is: Keep your life in motion—your planets a dynamic force in your personal solar system. If you master that technique, not only will you be truly living—you will enrich your life with the things that really matter.

Solar System Worksheets

These are duplicate forms, suitable for photocopying, of the Solar System Chart and other work materials for the Solar System Technique.

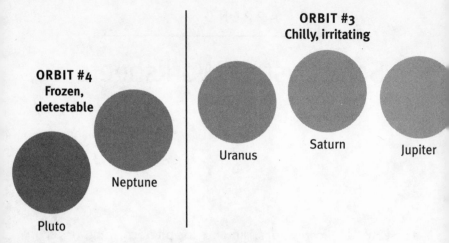

SOLAR SYSTEM CHART

This highly schematic drawing of our solar system shows the order of the planets by their distance from the sun—from hot Mercury, to warm Earth ("third rock from the sun"), out to frozen Pluto. Mark your personal solar system choices on a copy of this chart in relation to their distance from your *own* sun.

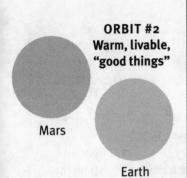

**ORBIT #2
Warm, livable,
"good things"**

Mars

Earth

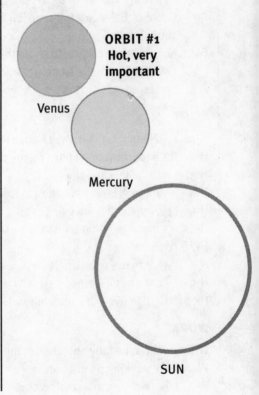

**ORBIT #1
Hot, very
important**

Venus

Mercury

SUN

SOLAR SYSTEM CHART

FAMILY

F-1. I want to be married.

F-2. I want a child.

F-3. I want a large family.

F-4. I'd like to be a stay-at-home parent, at least until my kids are older.

F-5. It's important that my spouse be extremely involved in family life, and not let his/her work take preference.

F-6. I'd like my spouse to be the primary stay-at-home parent.

F-7. I want to balance a full-time job with child rearing from the start.

F-8. My spouse and I should share the same religion and views.

F-9. I want to live in the same city as my parents and siblings.

F-10. I prefer to stay single.

HOME

H-1. I'd like to live in an older house that I can restore myself.

H-2. It's important that I have plenty of space.

H-3. I want to live in a city.

H-4. I want to grow my own herb garden.

H-5. I prefer small-town living.

H-6. It's important that I live very close to where I work.

H-7. I'd like a big yard.

H-8. I want to live in an apartment, with little or no upkeep.

H-9. I want a large kitchen.

H-10. I'd like to live in a community where I know my neighbors.

WORK

W-1. I want to be fully absorbed in my work.

W-2. I like working on my own.

W-3. I like working in a small group.

W-4. I want to work in a large company, with lots of options.

W-5. I'd like to be a manager and direct others.

W-6. I love generating new business.

W-7. I want a career that allows plenty of time for family.

W-8. I want to work at home.

W-9. I'd like a job that involves travel.

W-10. I want to own my own company.

SPIRITUAL/PHILOSOPHICAL

S-1. My religious affiliation is central to my life.

S-2. I consider myself a spiritual person, but do not practice a traditional religious observance.

S-3. I attend church or synagogue only on holidays.

S-4. I admire the spiritual wisdom of people like Deepak Chopra.

S-5. I want my children to be raised in a traditional religious framework.

S-6. It's important that members of my family and close friends share my religious beliefs and values.

S-7. I believe that a person can be moral regardless of his or her sexual codes, etc.

S-8. I believe we were all put on earth to help each other.

S-9. I believe in an afterlife.

S-10. I consider myself a secular humanist.

INTELLECTUAL/CULTURAL

I-1. I love to go to the opera, ballet, and theater.

I-2. It's important that I have time to read every day.

I-3. I enjoy having music playing in the background when I'm working or relaxing.

I-4. I regularly take classes to improve my skills or learn something new.

I-5. It's important that I have opportunities to travel abroad.

I-6. For relaxation I enjoy movies and television.

I-7.   I am bored by museums and the theater. I'm a doer, not a watcher.

I-8.   I am uncomfortable in foreign environments.

I-9.   I enjoy cultural events that involve activities with others, such as ethnic festivals and dances.

I-10. I enjoy salons or book groups where people share ideas.

ACTIVITIES/INTERESTS

A-1.   I love to garden.

A-2.   I want to act in a play.

A-3.   I enjoy tinkering around the house.

A-4.   I need to have pets.

A-5.   I like to take walks by myself.

A-6.   It's important to me that I always look my best.

A-7.   I prefer activities that take place outdoors.

A-8.   I'm very interested in artistic areas.

A-9.   I enjoy writing in my journal.

A-10. I love to shop.

FRIENDS/COMMUNITY

C-1.   It is important to me that I live near my friends.

C-2.   I want to be involved in politics.

C-3.   I am committed to being involved in helping the less fortunate in my community.

C-4.   My friends are spread out all over the world, and I want the opportunity to visit them.

C-5.   I enjoy being involved with others in a community of interests (professional, political, cultural).

C-6.   It's important to me that I know and am close to my neighbors.

C-7.   I want to live in a group community setting.

C-8.   Community isn't very important to me. I prefer being with my family.

C-9.   I enjoy having many friends and meeting new people.

C 10.   I value my privacy and need time alone.

HEALTH/PHYSICAL FITNESS

P-1.   Being fit is extremely important to me.

P-2.   I exercise every day.

P-3.   I am careful to eat a special diet for health.

P-4.   I enjoy being active, but I don't have a set exercise program.

P-5.   I don't think much about what I eat.

P-6.   I have health problems that limit my mobility.

P-7.   I need to have access to doctors and specialists.

P-8.   My body and my look are extremely important to me.

P-9.   Going to the gym and taking exercise classes are important parts of my life.

P-10.   I eat only organic foods.

FINANCIAL/MONEY

M-1.   Financial security is very important to me.

M-2.   I want to make enough money so I can do what I want—travel, buy nice clothes, have a country home, etc.

M-3.   I don't care about money as long as I have what I need.

M-4.   I enjoy taking risks and playing the stock market.

M-5.   It is very important that I save money for retirement.

M-6.   Saving money isn't that important to me.

M-7.   I would be willing to earn less money if I was doing what I truly enjoyed.

M-8.   I am solely responsible for my support and the support of others.

M-9.   I have a partner or family members who share expenses.

M-10. I prefer to have no credit card debt or loans.

SAMPLE SUN / MERCURY TABLE OF VALUES

ITEM	IDEAL	ACTUAL
Totals